B

es, firenadoes, b...
ashes, food allergies (adult onset)
nildren's ministry, drive-by
ng internal organs, no more
room, children that will never
lid 9 hrs of sleep, tingly hands,
giving wedding toasts, texting
ing, the home security installation
've been afraid of: tornadoes,
eeds preschool, plane crashes
people asking me to serve in
ootings, chronic hiccups, exploding
ackets in the SNL green room,
creaming, not getting a solid
wrs, tickborne illnesses, cancer,
he wrong person the wrong
uy seeing my passcode.

AFRAID OF ALL *the* THINGS

AFRAID OF ALL *the* THINGS

TORNADOES, CANCER, ADOPTION, AND OTHER STUFF YOU NEED THE GOSPEL FOR

SCARLET HILTIBIDAL

B&H
PUBLISHING GROUP

NASHVILLE, TENNESSEE

978-1-5359-0593-0

Published by B&H Publishing Group
Nashville, Tennessee

Dewey Decimal Classification: 152.4
Subject Heading: ANXIETY \ PHOBIAS \ FEAR

1 2 3 4 5 6 7 • 23 22 21 20 19

Dedicated to Brandon, my best friend, life coach, unpaid editor, "Wind Beneath My Wings" (why do you make me call you that?), omelette master, and keeper of the best comb-over east of the Mississippi.

ACKNOWLEDGMENTS

There are so many people I am thankful for. First off, I'm thankful for Jesus, who is the reason I have anything of value to say. His healing and provision in my life has been a miracle.

Brandon, thank you for loving me. Thank you for listening to all my words—verbal, nonverbal, text, Google Chat, sleep-talking, loud singing, cry-laughing, laugh-yelling, and aggressive sign languaging. I'm thankful that you are attentive to my words on all utilized mediums. Thank you for taking the time to read everything I write and make it better. Thank you for overlooking my flaws, keeping my secrets, fathering my children, and staying married to me even when I make my hand into a puppet and put it right next to your face when you're trying to read your dragon books. Thank you for telling me I'm pretty everyday. Thank you for being steady and true in a house full of "slapdash swooshing." You are the best person I know and I'm so in love with you.

Ever, Dewy, and Joy, being your mommy is the most incredible gift. Ever, thank you for being a kind, fun, resilient, patient helper. Thank you for making me smile and being Jesus to me in the moments I'm weak. You are a treasure to Daddy and me. Brooklyn (our little Dewy), thank you for making me laugh every day and for holding my neck while I wrote this book. If I could have made every page of this book blue, believe me, Baby, I would have. Joy, thank you for being magically sweet, for showing me what courage looks like, and bringing us joy every day. I love that I get to be your snuggler and food preparer and tucker-inner.

To my huge, wonderful family—my parents, my grandparents, my in-laws, I love you so much. Thank you for loving me in so many ways, many of which I've included in this book.

Aubrey, my biscuit, I'm so thankful God gave me a baby sister that would grow up to be my best friend. I always wanted daughters because I so loved having a sister. Thank you for being wise and loving and fun and continuing to point your big sister to the unchanging Jesus. You are a treasure to me.

Uncle Jimmy, UJ, you were a bright spot during the years I was confused and fatherless. You made me laugh and loved me and taught me weird-cool things about the string theory and the God particle and being "on LA time" and aliens, and I just love you. I want to love the kids God put in my life the way you have always loved me.

Janet Yates, you were the first person that made me think I could do this. My love for writing words became a future I dreamed about when you told me you believed in me. Thank you.

Jennifer Lyell, sitting across that big conference table with you when you made this dream come true was surreal. I couldn't quite believe you were even talking to me and I will never forget the things you said, the compassionate counsel, and meaningful encouragement. I'm very thankful for you.

To the team at B&H, oh my goodness, you are wonderful. Throughout the process of making this book, I brainstormed possible reasons for meetings, because I just love sitting and talking about Jesus with you. Ashley Gorman, Mary Wiley, Devin Maddox, Taylor Combs, Jenaye White, Michelle Burke, and everyone else, you are the sharpest, sweetest, best team in the world. Thank you for all you've done to make this book happen.

Eric Geiger, your family means the world to mine. Thank you for loving and supporting us for all these years and leading us closer to Christ and into situations that have changed our lives.

To my friends—Katie, Jana, Caroline, I love you. Thank you for feeling feelings with me and letting me do life with you. And of course, Beverly, Jenni, and Kaye. Thank you for being my go-to's when I'm having a baby, getting wheeled into surgery, sobbing or laughing hysterically, or noticing an octopus. Christy and Nicole, you are like sisters to me, my forever friends. My grandchildren will know your names (actually, they'll probably know MY names for you, Little Crust and Bump).

To my pastor, Josh Howerton, sitting under your teaching has changed my family forever. Thank you for pointing us to Jesus and for all the Hower-Hilti-Hangs and legendary group texts. Thank you for sending me Tim Keller sermon transcripts that I wanted to use as I wrote this book and for overlooking the GIFs I've sent you and your family in poor taste. We love you and your people so much.

And finally, thank you to my local gym. You watched my kids while I wrote this book. You didn't judge me for wearing workout clothes while sitting and eating chocolate directly in front of healthy people on treadmills. Or maybe you did judge me, but nevertheless, you watched my kids.

CONTENTS

PREFACE

When I got the email from B&H Publishing Group, saying that they wanted to meet with me about publishing this book, I literally dry heaved.

And then, we met. And then, they gave me a book contract. And then, I signed it, right at the kitchen table with my husband while my dirty kids ate mixed vegetables with their hands.

I laughed. I cried. I pinched myself. I pinched my husband. I got onto my daughters for pinching each other. We were all really excited. Writing this book was a lifelong dream.

I basically wrote the first draft when I was nine. Really. It's in the big wooden thing in my kitchen right now. It's forty pages of pure sadness, hand-written on notebook paper. It's kind of hilarious in hindsight, but each page is just one sad, scary thing after the other with a brief respite in "Chapter 8." Those pages read, "I also have some good things in my life. Like, I hardly ever get sick . . . and I have lots of friends like a thirty-four-year-old named Harris, Betty Fanning (my mom's TV agent), and my grandparents."

And then, back to the worries. Divorce. Dog death. Bad haircut.

I was a broken and scared nine-year-old. I mean, *everything* scared me. I didn't yet know that Jesus is the only answer. I just knew I wanted to write books. I thought maybe that dream would fix things.

But between scribbling on notebook paper at nine and signing a real book contract at thirty-one, I got to learn that no publisher's opinion and no dream come true can give me what I really want.

Somewhere along the way, I learned that I've always had a deeper dream. Writing about fear could never conquer fear. My heart longed for perfect Love to cast it out.

Before I was a nine-year-old aspiring author, and even before the foundation of the world, I had a need and Jesus had the answer.

Jesus was the answer.

Jesus is the dream.

Getting to publish this book has been surreal. I've spent the past sixteen months pinching pretty much everyone. But the reason I was even able to write this book in the first place is because God gave me the grace to find out, before this dream came true, that the dream couldn't do what I wanted it to.

Only Jesus could.

What He says tells me who I am. What He did decides who I'll be.

So I'm thrilled and in shock and excited to share with you all, stories from my life and how Jesus has saved me from my deepest struggle. How He's taken someone who was defined by panic and created a new person with the peace of God.

Guys, my dream came true! In addition to that, I got to write this book! There aren't enough exclamation points in all the world.

INTRODUCTION

I've lived scared as long as I can remember.

Gearing up for my first day of kindergarten, I had great expectations. I lived in Weston, Connecticut, which is beautiful and foresty and full of thin women who don't wear makeup and retired songwriters and ticks and windy roads.

I was only five, but I'd seen other girls. Other girls wore dresses. So I wanted to wear a dress on my first day of school. But my mom had already picked out an outfit for me that was "chic" and "classy" and "sophisticated."

It wasn't those things.

Only an eighty-year-old man would appreciate this getup. Tucked-in argyle vest? Starched dress shirt? Charcoal, pleated tuxedo pants? Seriously?

Look at that photo again. It's real.

In hindsight, my mom was about as laid-back as she was a fan of me wearing man suits. She probably would have let me skip the argyle had I asked. But I was little. Little people don't always know that asking is an option.

So I started kindergarten in a man suit. It was scary, but I was also dealing with bigger, scarier problems. My little life was falling apart. Divorce and a new dad and a new home. As my security evaporated, so did my peace.

My fear didn't disappear when I left behind kindergarten and men's clothes. The fear only morphed and changed as I got older. But I always had things to be afraid of. I've had seasons in adulthood when I couldn't stop hyperventilating.

I had a black widow phase.

A sinkhole phase.

A rare infectious disease phase.

A bad guys phase.

A pretty major tornado phase.

My husband jokes regularly about my frequent YouTube deep dives into tornado destruction videos.

"Whatcha doin'?"

"Watching a tornado swallow a warehouse in China three years ago."

"Why?"

"Because a tornado swallowed a warehouse in China three years ago."

In my young adult years, I explored all the short-term solutions I could find. Boys and bulimia and good grades and achievements. All of it left me feeling more anxious and more guilty and more restless.

So I tried more things.

I did the therapies and the medicines and the self-help books. They helped for a while, and for some people, they really are needed for the long haul (I get into my thoughts on medicine in chapter 4). But for some reason, with me, nothing lasted. Nothing really changed.

And then I changed.

I became a Christian shortly after I stopped wearing argyle vests, but, in a lot of ways, I didn't start thinking like a Christian and feeling like a Christian until about seven years ago. I had what I call my gospel awakening. Jesus started to mean more for more reasons in more moments. The Jesus who had only felt like the answer for salvation became the answer for everything. The Jesus who had always been the hope for my afterlife became my hope for after breakfast. I started to see that His work on the cross, which I had always known would make God smile at me someday, had already given me God's smile today. Right now.

I want to show you how true peace came when I started holding the gospel up to my fears. Here's what I mean and what this book is about.

In light of the gospel, I saw that my fears, though many and rampant, do not define me. We'll look at this in section 1. I learned that my fears, though scary and some-times rooted in real possibility, will not defeat me. That is the thrust of section 2. And I remembered that my fears, though heavy and hard to shake, are not forever. That is the focus of section 3.

The gospel tells me I can't fix myself.

The gospel tells me I can't protect myself.

But the gospel tells me I can rest, knowing that Jesus walked into this broken, sad, scary place to rescue me and love me and cast out my fear. And He did and He does and He will.

Calm is found in the already finished work of Christ.

I don't know when you learned that you live in a broken, sad place, but I know you know. I don't know if you own pleated tuxedo pants (I pray you don't) or when and how your sense of security evaporated, but I know it did.

Jesus wants you to have it back. But only in Him and only because of Him. And, really, that's the only way we *can* have it back. Anything else depends on us and I think we know how that goes by now.

We dress like grandpas. He speaks and storms are stilled. We run from spiders. He demolishes death. We panic over future failure. He never fails and He holds the future.

When hyperventilaters, danger avoiders, cancer finders, and sinkhole expecters grasp that, we can echo the psalmist with certainty, "The LORD is on my side; I will not fear. What can man do to me?" (Ps. 118:6 ESV).

Before turning the page, please take one last look at Grandfather Scarlet. Thank you for letting me share my story.

Section 1

MY FEARS
DO NOT
DEFINE ME

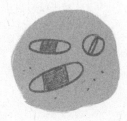

Chapter One

MY HYPOCHONDRIAC COLLAPSE IN AISLE SIX

• • •• • • • • • • • •• • • •

Do you know what it feels like when your appendix ruptures? The burst of hot, searing pain in the lower right-hand side of your abdomen? The punch of the invisible spear that pierces you so suddenly and so acutely that your feet go out from under you like you slipped on black ice and your body contorts into the fetal position faster than a final death rattle? Do you know that pain?

Yeah, I don't know what that feels like either. My appendix is holding strong.

But ever since the moment I learned, as a five-year-old, that appendicitis was a thing during a casual skimming of *Madeline*, I just knew it was my fate. That and all the other ailments and grave situations I'd ever heard of. Cancer. AIDS. Black Widow bites. Severe bee allergies. Eczema. Tumors. Chronic Hiccups.

I never thought about what the afterwards of an appendix rupture would be like—the healing and the life-going-on part. I was consumed by the horror of the event—the organ going rogue, the blood escaping inside my body, the bad and the scary. I was always bracing myself for it, so much so that I was convinced I could feel it happening.

FIRST MEMORY OF FEAR

My pediatrician preferred the phrase "nervous stomach," but the appendix pains arrived shortly after my parents got divorced. My mom then reconnected with her high school sweetheart, Paul, a Miami-Dade SWAT cop with impossibly large deltoids, a black fanny pack with a gun inside, the ability to get every single coin in the first level of Super Mario Brothers but somehow still not win, and the chops to play "When You Say Nothing at All" and every other favorite song you can think of on the piano, by ear. I think they dated for about a year, but it felt like one second before wedding bells rang. We were a happy family of four, my mom, my new dad, me, and my rapidly fading appendix.

One day Paul was driving us to Circle W Ranch down a road he called "Bloody 27," and my appendix definitely felt rupturish.

"Paul . . . why is this road called Bloody 27?" I asked.

He probably answered by recalling detailed cop stories he had lived through involving "victims" that he witnessed "being extracted from automobile wreckage, so it's very important to always wear your safety belt."

He was and is a cautious and loving father who, to this day, still capitalizes on every opportunity to remind us about the importance of safety belts.

Circle W Ranch was some land Paul's late father owned, with cows and horses and an orange grove in Ona, Florida. Those four-hour drives felt so long, and I hated it more when we'd drive in the dark. There were no city lights or fire trucks or medical buildings anywhere in sight. As a kid who'd grown up in big cities, I found comfort in a crowd. More people around meant more helpers if you needed them. More safety. So, you can imagine how my appendix felt about country living, even just visiting. Somewhere, at some point, I'd heard a commercial for a horror movie or something that said, ". . . where no one can hear you scream . . ." That was, to me, the essence of country life.

And that's what this place, Circle W Ranch, was. A breeding ground for bad guys that would probably be the end of me. I imagined them hiding behind every orange tree and every fence row and every cow, all wearing the *Scream* mask, obviously.

Sure, there was space to run and the farmhand, Randy, would cut oranges in this cool way where you could just suck the juice right out. But there were also bugs everywhere and dirt and cows and horses that were definitely always trying to eat me, and like I said before, a striking absence of nearby helpers available to rescue me from whoever and whatever was hiding behind the cows.

My decomposing appendix and I listened as Paul and my mom were chatting in the car. I white-knuckled my car door through every stomach cramp. As we sped by a patch of trees, I saw two bright headlights, which plainly were part of a UFO that had definitely found me in Florida and surely planned to abduct me right from the car. All those things I'd heard about in my "stranger danger" speeches, those aliens were about to do them to me right now.

Thankfully, aliens didn't threaten my life that day, but I thought my appendix did.

"Mommy, which side is the right side again?"

She showed me and said, "Your appendix is fine."

No, it isn't. I just knew it wasn't. She couldn't feel what I was feeling. She hadn't researched appendicitis symptoms from *World Book* in the school library as thoroughly and as recently as I had. I was certain that it was only a matter of time until mine exploded, and now was my time.

Paul backed the car into a spot at Winn Dixie. (Free Police Officer Tidbit: Backing in is the safest way to park a car.) He and his fanny pack/gun carrier escorted me and my mom into the grocery store. I shuffled through the automatic doors, clutching my stomach, feeling trapped in my own perishing body, determined to meet death with grace in this Winn Dixie.

I wanted to escape the panic I felt inside. I wanted to laugh and skip down the aisles and beg for things in the toy section like a regular kid. But, as we walked in, it jabbed me again. The sharp abdominal pain. I held my fingers up into to Ls to double check, *WHICH SIDE IS MY RIGHT?* Sure enough, the pain was still on the right, just like little, redheaded Madeline, and I collapsed right there on the grocery store floor. Paul says it was aisle six.

Was my appendix rupturing? No. No, it was not. Does my family still talk about my false appendix collapse in aisle six? Yes. Yes, they do.

After a night in a middle-of-nowhere hospital, getting poked and being hooked up to beeping monitors, we were told, by a new doctor in a new city, that I was, as always, a picture of health and that I should maybe try to calm down and stop reading the encyclopedia so much.

LIFE BEFORE FEAR

Before Circle W and appendix pains, I grew up in green rooms. My mom was a cast member on *Saturday Night Live*, which I didn't know was a big deal until I grew up and people told me it was a big deal. We lived in Connecticut because *SNL* was, of course, ". . . live from New York . . ." and my mom wanted to live outside of the city. She commuted to work by train, and I was often with my stay-at-home biological dad/part-time magician or with the comedians, eating lemon pound cake from the food table backstage.

I remember a lot of fun things about the sets I grew up on. People were friendly and knew my name and there were delicious, interesting foods on platters and fancy juices on fancy ice in fancy buckets.

Most all of my fuzzy memories of that time were of fun. Those jelly packets on the food table on set that I'd lick right out of the packet. The pads of paper in my mom's office that said NBC on every page. I'd write on every sheet and it was okay because next time I was there, a new one would appear. I watched Adam Sandler jump through a fake glass window from backstage, and then I kissed the TV screen when I saw him on it later.

And I spent hours bouncing on our trampoline. And I had a swing set with a fort where I'd color, and I had the bus stop where I'd wait for the kindergarten bus that was surrounded by happy yellow flowers. I couldn't have dreamed up anything better. So much laughter. So much paper. So much jelly.

And nothing to be afraid of.

SOMETHING TO BE AFRAID OF

But then we went to a barbecue. I thought it was just a normal barbecue on a normal day. There was a lake, I think, and someone was grilling burgers. And my mom whisked me away from the party to a sterile office building that had a big copy machine and so many colors of Wite-Out. I didn't know Wite-Out came in different colors. Mom and a man I'd never seen were speaking in hushed tones about papers and legal fees and I was painting pink Wite-Out onto a piece of copy paper.

I didn't understand what was happening. I didn't know that I was about to learn that this world is a broken place. I didn't know that marriages end or that relationships vanish.

I had no idea it was even possible to leave your home and never go back.

But we left the office building and boarded a plane to Los Angeles, just me and Mom. And then, *poof*, we were gone.

And I remember eating white rice at Teru Sushi and realizing my stomach hurt. It never really stopped.

One morning there was a daddy longlegs perched on the toilet paper roll, so I couldn't go to the bathroom for hours because I didn't know what to do. And it hurt so bad to hold it in, but what were my options? Dad had disappeared, so who was going to get the spider? Did moms get spiders? If anyone's mom could get a spider, it would have been mine, but I wasn't sure if girls had the ability to do that sort of thing.

My dad was now gone, but not in the way I was used to at the children's birthday parties where he—yes, my dad the magician and fire-eater—would wear a turban with a giant plastic gemstone in the middle. He wasn't "gone" like he was when he'd shut a flimsy plastic door and then step out the back of an even flimsier chamber. He was gone-gone and farther away than I could comprehend. And I was afraid. My stomach hurt, my life was weird, and no one was stronger than the spiders.

And Madeline sure didn't do me any favors.

AFRAID OF THE BIBLE

Before my family fell apart, during my jelly-eating, Adam-Sandler-TV-kissing phase, I wasn't even aware that I lived in a spiritual world. I knew we were churchgoers. I knew we prayed. I'd probably memorized a few Bible verses by that point. But Jesus wasn't real to me. What *was* real was this foreign life I found myself in, one where the comfort of home can go away unannounced and a meeting that seems to be about how awesome colored Wite-Out is can end with a one-way ticket to Daddy-Longlegs-ville.

One night my mom sat at the foot of my bed and pulled out the little blue leather Bible that had my name engraved in gold "Scarlet Eventoff."

She flipped to Joshua 1:9 and read it out loud, "Haven't I commanded you: be strong and courageous? Do not be afraid or discouraged, for the LORD your God is with you wherever you go."

She already knew I had a fear problem. When your child is frequently asking you if you've nailed down a detailed earthquake safety plan and each passing bee is a world-ending tragedy, it's pretty clear there's an issue.

She grabbed one of my colored pencils and underlined that verse and wrote the date beside it and told me it was one of her favorites.

The thing about anxiously wired people though, is that our minds can twist everything—even comfort, even Truth—into something else to be afraid of.

That verse, which was—though I didn't know it—pointing directly at the One who could heal my wounds, became a weight I started carrying around with me.

God COMMANDS me to be strong? God REQUIRES me to be courageous? But, I'm not strong. I'm not even close to courageous. I'm weak and I'm scared. I'm afraid and I'm sad. I literally won't go to the bathroom within a hundred yards of a daddy longlegs. How can He love me and be "with me" if He's perfect and I do and feel everything wrong?

I don't know if you have ever been afraid of the Bible, but it is a real thing. I was a regular in the back row, right side, church pew every Sunday at First Baptist Church of Pasadena, but the Bible wasn't a comfort to me. The gospel wasn't "good news" to me. I thought it was only good news for the people who were doing it right. It was only good for the people who had that peace the Bible kept talking about.

The gospel didn't make me feel loved. It made me feel like a failure.

GOOD NEWS FOR SCARED PEOPLE

That verse my mom showed me in my Los Angeles canopy bed that night on Lookout Mountain wasn't just a random quote or platitude or historical account I needed to memorize. It was God speaking to Joshua, who had just seen his leader, his friend, Moses, die.

God told Joshua to take over as leader of the Israelites. God told Joshua to lead His people into the enemy-occupied Promised Land. To that, I would say a polite, "no thank you." I'm uncomfortable with the leadership required to send out a group text about who is bringing the soccer team snack, so I can't imagine the type of fear Joshua must have been feeling, being given such a huge responsibility from God.

But in verse 5, God said to Joshua, "I will be with you, just as I was with Moses. I will not leave you or abandon you."

God's promise wasn't that Joshua's life would be like an afternoon on the couch with Hulu and hummus. God knew there was real war in Joshua's future. And His dialogue with Joshua wasn't a, "YOU'D BETTER DO A GOOD JOB BECAUSE YOU'VE GOT MOSES' SHOES TO FILL. YOU'D BETTER BE BRAVE, JOSHUA. YOU'D BETTER BE STRONG. OH MAN, JOSH. YOU WON'T BELIEVE HOW I CAN GET WHEN MY MOSES REPLACEMENTS AREN'T BRAVE ENOUGH."

No.

God said to Joshua, "Do not be afraid or discouraged." It was a comfort, not a condemnation, because immediately after that, God said, ". . . for the LORD your God is with you wherever you go."

His promise was His presence. And His presence brings peace. God's presence brings peace, but it is so easy to read the events of our lives like they are a message from God saying, "I CAN'T EVEN BELIEVE HOW MUCH YOU ARE THE WORST." He didn't talk that way to Joshua. He doesn't talk that way to you. And He wasn't talking that way to me when I hid from His Word in the Hollywood Hills.

Despite the happy childhood trappings I enjoyed—having a comfortable home and a mom and a new dad who put me through Christian school and sat through all my 400-hour recitals and award ceremonies, and bought me important necessities like dancing scarves and hamster-replacement-hamsters—I woke up each day, not trusting my home to stay in the same place, not expecting people to stay in my life, not believing my body would do its job to keep me alive another day, and not trusting that my faith was enough to save me. The only things I trusted were the world to be scary and my appendix to explode before the hour was out.

GOD LOVE JOSHUAS AND MIDDLE SCHOOLERS

In eighth grade, I had a light-up bracelet, and I had crushes on boys with shaved heads who were a year younger and at least four inches shorter than I was (those were my prerequisites), and I made a really weird sound when I laughed. Up to that point, one of my proudest moments was winning an award at school for "worst laugh."

But let's talk about my hair really quick.

You need to know first, that shortly after this photo was taken, my hair became orange for the next ten years, because I wanted to be blonde, but I wasn't allowed to dye my hair, so I found a loophole, which I think was some type of hydrogen peroxide spray, called Sun-In. So, in short, the visual experience in this picture only got worse.

Secondly, those were the bangs I had. Yes, voluntarily. Why this was the look I chose and executed during what everyone knows is the most intensely vulnerable stage of life is something I still don't understand. *Why, little Scarlet? Why force that forehead framing on an already wounded world?*

One other thing I will never understand is why I thought that the perfect, essence-capturing AOL Instant Messenger name for the person photographed above was HippieChick86. Then, soon after, GlitteryPomPom. Followed closely by LilWindmil. What does that even mean? I could go on and psychoanalyze my string of subsequent AOL Instant Messenger names, but that seems unhelpful.

I think the obvious takeaway here is that I was very unsure about who I was. This is true of almost every middle schooler I've ever heard of, but the thing is, I was panicked about it. Terrified, really. I was a crooked-banged, chubby girl with one friend and my longed-for identities were plastered all over AOL.

I wanted to be a hippie, but I didn't know any. I wanted to be a "chick" because that sounded simultaneously cool and casual, and cool and casual people probably aren't scared of everything. I wanted to be a glittery, pom-pom-shaking, popular cheerleader. Those are fun. Apparently, I also wanted to be a little windmill? With only one "L" on the end? I don't know.

But here's what started happening. I would either pursue these identities and fail at them (hippie fail; cool chick extra fail; windmill with one L, obviously, that didn't pan out), or I would pursue and actually achieve the identity (glittery cheerleader) and still be afraid of the world. Whether I became the thing I was longing to be or not, the anxiety didn't go away. I was still afraid. I was still wondering if I was glittery enough or smart enough or funny enough or safe enough. Even as a, wait for it . . . CHAMPION CHEERLEADER, my life was still unpredictable. My heart was still in pain. I still wasn't safe.

In short, I was a mess. The GPA could never get high enough. The cheer skirts were never flattering enough. And the praise from classmates and teachers was fleeting.

But God saved me. Glitter, jitters, bangs, and all.

That's the person He came for at a local church in Burbank, California—that orange-haired, desperately nervous, attention-seeking wreck.

It happened during an amateur play about women finding Jesus on death row. At fourteen years old, I was still years away from really understanding grace, but I knew that I met Jesus in that church that day. And I knew, somehow, that He loved me. It still sounds absurd, eighteen years later. Jesus loved awkward, crooked-banged, nail-biting, boyfriend-less, wannabe me.

After that play, I cried and cried and felt, for the first time, that maybe Jesus really did want me. It was stunning to me, watching that death row play, that He could love people who had broken *all* the rules. He loved people who broke what I thought were the *most serious* rules. As a panic-button-person, I was totally about the rules and I wanted to be saved from them. I understood at least some of who Jesus was. I understood my need for Him.

I understood I couldn't keep the rules and that He knew I couldn't, which is why He kept them for me and then paid the price for all my breaking of them.

But.

As I started to walk with Him, I fell back into the belief that it was all up to me to be good enough. I thought, *now that salvation has happened, I'd better do a good job of being a Christian.* I shifted, maybe without my knowing, from feeling saved from the rules to feeling saved by the rules.

I suspect a lot of people live that way. So many have lived, like me, under the faulty belief system that, yes, we need grace, but it's up to us and our strength and our will-power and our God-infused goodness to "walk the walk." It's up to us to earn His favor.

I believed I could be saved by grace, but that, in order to be approved by God, I had to live in near-perfect obedience for the rest of my days. I also believed that the more orange my hair was, the closer it was to blonde. Neither of those beliefs were rooted in reality and neither of them delivered.

GROWING UP CAN KILL YOU

Thankfully, I grew out of those phases and fears into ones that were less bangs-centric. But even my more "mature" quests for security and fulfillment fell flat. I wanted to marry the sweet football player I dated throughout high school as soon I turned eighteen because maybe *then,* I'd stop being afraid. Maybe *then* I wouldn't have to worry about missing out on love or missing out on family or missing out on things I might not even know I was missing. Maybe *then,* I could rest and be happy. Maybe *then* I'd feel loved and safe.

Back then, my goals looked a little something like this:

Goal #1: Make my boyfriend love me more and more with each passing day and with such single-minded devotion that we will be married before the ink dries on our high school diplomas.

Goal #2: Get straight A's and smile a lot so teachers and students and parents and strangers will admire and adore me with a fierce and inexplicable passion. Use of the word "special" is preferred.

My parents were concerned about the seriousness of my high school relationship. Maybe it was the lengthy love songs I'd compose and sing at full volume at the piano everyday after school while also crying. Maybe it was the not-a-secret graph I kept in my school planner, detailing how much my guy seemed to like me each day. Whatever it was, Paul would often say, "Scarlet . . . you're tunnel-visioned. You could be focused on so many other things . . ."

But that only meant I had to start the song over.

It didn't work, though. We didn't get married, and even when I thought we might, security always felt just out of reach.

A few years later, I met Brandon, the man I *did* marry. I met him at a church plant he started with my former youth pastor. He sang about Jesus from the stage and had actual tears come out when he prayed, and he wrote—I'm not making this up—Shakespearean sonnets to get the youth group kids to come to events.

After service one day, I bounced up to him and said, all in one breath, "You are so good with words! I love writing. I'm an English major! Want to race to the swing set over there?"

We ended up racing, and I got a job at the church and we fell in love. I wanted to be prettier and cooler and more lovable. Maybe then, this amazing, godly man would keep liking me. I was so afraid of losing a relationship.

And suddenly, I was an anorexic/bulimic church secretary. I was shocked and confused to be battling a big, humiliating "lifestyle sin." I was a rule expert. I was a worry pro. How had I ever stopped fearing rule breaking long enough for this to happen? Of course, I'd just traded the fear of not being good enough for the fear of not being pretty enough. I was still afraid every minute. Maybe more than ever.

Somehow, during those years, I managed to not die. Brandon and I got married and I suffered in secret and begged God for healing. But rather than healing me like "Poof," the way I wanted Him to, He continually directed me to Proverbs 28:13. "The one who conceals his sins will not prosper, but whoever confesses and renounces them will find mercy." I didn't want to confess because it was such an ugly sin, but that verse kept coming after me until I did it. It's been a decade now since I confessed and He healed me that very day and it went away instantly. His Word led me to the greatest moment of freedom I've ever known.

God graciously kept on giving me freedom from my fears and failures. But it felt like I would just barely escape a former fear and a former phase only to find a fresh one following right behind. Even when I overcame, I was a nervous, sleepless, shaking wreck.

So I had kids.

In the next phase, I was a young mom, fresh off of a miscarriage, who was certain my healthy newborn baby wouldn't make it to her next birthday. I just knew that she'd be the first baby in the history of Earth to be absorbed by a twin she didn't have in a womb she was no longer in. It's never too late to be absorbed by your nonexistent twin. Or maybe she would accidentally fall out of her crib and register for the wrong college while I was going to the bathroom. I kept the hand sanitizer companies in business and I'm pretty sure the term "helicopter parent" was coined by someone who saw me "relaxing" during that time.

It would be hard to pinpoint the moment it happened, but somewhere between neurotically studying to get perfect grades in high school and college—willing myself to live off of four ounces of tuna fish a day in my first church job—and letting the worries of motherhood consume me in my early adult years, these restless behaviors and fears I jumped to and from and freaked out in weren't just things I suffered through.

They became who I thought I was.

Nervous wreck. Leg bouncer. Nail biter. Hyperventilator. Hypochondriac. Clingy Girlfriend. The Foodless One. Worried Wife and New Parent of Utmost Panic. These were the identities I cycled through, driven by the fears that ate me up. As soon as I found freedom from one, I'd latch onto another. Never resting. Always striving. Fighting to the death to save myself.

The crazy thing about it all is that *Jesus loved me*. Even then, He loved me. I wish I'd believed it.

He loved me *before* I trusted Him. Before I gave up food obsessions and baby obsessions and boy obsessions. He loved me, afraid of everything and winning at nothing.

> But God demonstrates his own love for us
> in this: While we were still sinners, Christ
> died for us. (Rom. 5:8 NIV)

MY GOSPEL AWAKENING

After all the phases, the pain, the repentance, the freedom, and the living to fear another day, I was still functioning, in many ways, like I was lost. I was still very much a slave to fear. I was, as my home church calls it, over-churched and under-gospeled.

I didn't think it was possible to know the Lord, to study Him, talk to Him, be changed by Him, and not really UNDERSTAND His core message.

But that was me. Then, God gave me a gospel awakening moment.

Brandon was pastoring a campus of a megachurch in Miami that had, probably, twenty pastors in total. So I was invited to a "pastors' wives retreat" in the Florida Keys.

Most of the wives with babies left their kids with dads or grandparents, but I knew no one could take care of my baby, Ever, like I could, so instead of savoring crab cakes and encouragement from like-minded women, I was burping my colicky newborn in hallways by myself and bounce-pacing in one of the bathrooms with her at 2 a.m. so I wouldn't wake up the other women.

Those early days of motherhood were some of the most terrifying of my life. I wasn't afraid of being a bad mom. I was afraid of absurd things. I was afraid of other people holding her and not being gentle enough. I was afraid of getting carjacked and watching a black market baby seller drive off with her every time I left the house.

And there I was in this circle of calm, happy women.

We were sitting in a big group in a borrowed beach house, discussing parenting. The older pastors' wives were schooling us young ones on discipline strategies and behavior-shaping methods. One after another, these older, wiser women rattled off the names of books I should have already had memorized and disciplinary tactics I was supposed to have already started implementing at least at the moment of conception, if not sooner.

I tried to hang on to every word while also trying to stoke my shame and keep my baby's new found "Ba ba ba ba ba ba" skill to an unnoticeable whisper by way of bouncing and shushing.

Then, this woman I barely knew named Elizabeth, the newest of the pastors' wives with big earrings, blonde hair, and sparkly eyes opened her mouth and changed my life.

We were just a bunch of women talking time-outs and then Elizabeth started talking and exploded my worldview and the entire foundation of my religious life in three minutes flat.

She leaned back in her chair and said something like, "I don't focus on trying to get my kids to behave perfectly. They're not going to and that's not my goal. My goal is to raise kids who know how much they need Jesus and help them see that Jesus is enough."

She continued, "When my husband and I argue, we do it in front of them. And then we apologize in front of them. We show them what repentance and forgiveness look like. Then, I pray, and I ask God to forgive me. And I ask my husband to forgive me. And I ask my kids to forgive me. I don't hide my sin from them. I let them see it. And I tell them that I need Jesus every second of every day."

She presented a lifestyle and a goal I hadn't yet considered. One where fear can't speak because Jesus has already spoken. One where rest is found in what Jesus has done, not something I am capable of trying or failing at.

She unlocked the idea that I didn't have to be afraid of standing before God on Judgment Day. I didn't have to be scared of dying before I memorized the Minor Prophets or before faith-healing a child long dead from appendicitis. She presented me with this thought, that I could rest in the work of Jesus. That I could smile, no matter what was before me, because God was constantly smiling at me already, because of what Jesus has done, already.

For a terrified new mom who was a current or former fearer of just about everything, this felt like winning the lottery. My heart couldn't believe its luck. She wasn't pointing to a formula, but to a cross. She wasn't saying "do," but "DONE." She wasn't saying "you," she was saying "Jesus." And it wasn't like I had never heard His name before, but it had never sounded so sweet. It had never sounded so complete. Jesus and His death and victory were suddenly, clearly, overwhelmingly enough.

God used Elizabeth's words to rewire my brain, melt my heart with a gospel epiphany, and free me from living in fear.

I saw then as I've seen a hundred times since, that my fears cannot define me. My fears, my failures, my phases, real and imagined and everything in between, do not get to say who I am. They can't. Because Jesus already did. He rose from the dead with new names for me. Forgiven. Approved. Loved. Daughter. Heir. Friend.

This is what Elizabeth helped me see that I hope finds its way to your heart. Fear can't name you if, through Jesus, that job has already been filled. So settle down, look at the cross, and double-check your pretty-okay appendix. The gospel is real. We have nothing to fear.

Chapter Two

AIRPLANE SPRINGS

• • • • • • • • • • • • • • •

Growing up, I was a frequent flyer, bouncing between LAX and LGA and MIA. I was an in-flight magazines collector. I preferred my peanuts individually wrapped. I could recite the safety procedures better than the flight attendants themselves.

"Um, excuse me, ma'am? I believe you forgot to include that federal law prohibits, not only disabling or destroying a smoke detector, but also 'tampering with' one. You're welcome. Let's not have a smoke detector tampering on this flight, please."

Even after our big move to Miami, my mom continued to pursue acting, so we'd spend months every year in Los Angeles for pilot season. Paul ended up transitioning from SWAT Team Officer to Police Helicopter Pilot. So he spent every work night flying and then, when my mom and sister and I would fly to LA for extended periods of time, he'd fly out every other week or so to see us.

What I'm trying to say is that, as a family unit, we spent a lot of time up in the air. A lot of time trying not to spill plastic cups of V8. A lot of time drawing beards and mustaches on all the people in all the magazines because all that was playing on the airplane screens was *Roseanne*.

I have fuzzy early memories (reinforced by family members) of walking up and down the aisles of American Airlines flights, introducing myself to adults, and departing the plane with a new list of lady friends and friend boys.

Flying wasn't something I was afraid of, because I didn't know there was any reason to be afraid.

Then, I learned that planes crash.

Sometimes, instead of flying, they stop flying and explode. When I heard that, my flippant flying attitude while perusing the plane for friendly grown-ups, turned to complete panic and tears and gasping into airsick bags because I'd seen it done in cartoons. I was glued to the seat, too scared to move.

Surely, I was about to die at every takeoff and every landing and every *beep-boop ding-ding* and seat-belt sign flashing and "Please take your seats. We're experiencing some minor turbulence."

"Mommy, turbulence means we're dying, right?"

One particular day I was crying my way onto another five-hour flight with my mom, and she was trying to talk me down. I could just feel someone tampering with the smoke detector. Then, like an angel from heaven, a seasoned flight attendant leaned over and put her face level with mine.

"Oh Dear, you don't have to be afraid of crashing. Don't you know there are springs on the bottom of airplanes? If they fall out of the sky, the giant springs bounce them right back up into the air! There's nothing to be afraid of!"

And that was all I needed. One sweet, sweet lie.

That lie bought me years of tranquil air travel. Years of one less thing to be afraid of.

Sometimes believing lies just feels better. We believe a lot of lies that pretend to protect our hearts from the things we fear. It might start with airplane springs, but dishonest hopes can be found everywhere.

As I got older, I started believing that I had all sorts of control over my life and future. It sounded something like, "Well, if I never drive through *that* neighborhood . . ."

"Well, if I live in a town where that spider isn't found . . ."

"Well, as long as I sit behind the driver, I'll be fine, because studies show that a driver is more likely to protect their own side of the car in the event of an accident . . ."

"Well, if I walk everywhere, I'll never need a car and I'll never be trapped in that car if I ever drive into a pond while sneezing, because you know, you can't sneeze and keep your eyes open at the same time . . ."

And these little lies really did give me a weird sort of comfort from *certain* fears. I didn't fear airplanes for a couple years, because hello, springs! I'd stop obsessing over certain spiders that had never been seen within a 100-mile radius of my area code. Because, come on, now. Who, in their right mind, is going to trap a Black Widow in a jar 400 miles away and release it right in front of my house? Actually, did someone do that? Just move on.

The being comforted by lies thing was especially true as I grew older and developed more say over where I lived and what I did and how I traveled.

So lies did bring me some comfort. But I didn't live with *peace.*

More life freedom didn't actually equal more heart peace, because I couldn't escape the reality that nothing I have control over in life can keep a happy barbecue from becoming a day of divorce.

Nothing I do or don't do can keep a truck carrying hazardous materials from exploding next to me on the interstate. I can't keep my people from getting cancer. I've not yet figured out how to keep a West-Nile-virus-carrying-mosquito from finding me right now.

Getting closer to home, nothing I have control over can keep me from miscarrying or getting a late-night phone call that my sister has been in a car accident, or being told by my mom while in a ballet studio bathroom stall that her doctor found a lump.

There are no lies and no preventative measures that can keep us from pain and suffering. Airplane springs are not a thing. "Safety," honestly, is not a thing. We're not safe here, in this broken place. Not a single one of us.

But we don't have to be afraid.

I will both lie down and sleep in peace, for
you alone, LORD, make me live in safety.
(Ps. 4:8)

Anytime we tell our hearts that we have the power to
make ourselves safe, we lie. We don't have "live in safety"
powers. We lie down. God makes safe. Anything else is as
made up as airplane springs.

• • • • •

When considering the psalmst's words "I will fear no
evil" in Psalm 23, Charles Spurgeon said, "The worst evils
of life are those which do not exist except in our imagina-
tion. If we had no troubles but real troubles, we should not
have a tenth part of our present sorrows. We feel a thousand deaths in fearing one, but the psalmist was cured of
the disease of fearing."[1]

I think a common Christian hang-up is knowing we
can be "cured of the disease of fearing" and yet struggling
to rest. Struggling to trust. Struggling with fear and then
fearing the fear we feel.

Rationalizing and common sense don't work with irra-
tional fears. I mean, listen—you can try . . .

You can remind yourself that plane crashes are few and
far between. You can pore over articles about their rarity
and tape the statistics onto your refrigerator to remind
yourself that the odds of dying in a plane crash are 1 in 29.4
million. You can try to comfort yourself by meditating on

how often you drive in your car and how much more dangerous driving is than flying. (Wait . . . that's not helpful.)

But it won't help, you guys. Because, remember? You've YouTube-binged plane crash footage. And you watch the news. And even if you've already sworn off the news because what is scarier than the news, you catch glimpses of it in the Facebook sidebar or on the elliptical TV screen next to you at the gym. You know that plane crashes *do* happen and you know that if you get on a plane, it will probably happen to you.

So you, like Spurgeon says, feel a thousand plane crashes in fearing one. One out of 29.4 million.

But God's Word directs our focus away from 29.4 million and rightly sets it on One. There is One who has ultimate power. There is One who has total control. There is One who has immeasurable love for you.

> See what great love the Father has given us
> that we should be called God's children—
> and we are! . . . (1 John 3:1)

What are we scared of? Planes falling out of the sky. But whose children are we? The One who literally made the sky. And He doesn't just know us, He LOVES us.

I love Matthew Henry's commentary on the first few verses of 1 John 3. Henry writes, "Little does the world know of the happiness of the real follower of Christ. Little does the world think that these poor, humble, despised ones, are favourites of God, and will dwell in heaven."[2]

Favourites of God. Isn't that wild? Especially with the old English spelling.

Rather than seeking the cure to your fears in favorable (favourable) statistics or sparkly distractions, you can be "cured of the disease of fearing" in the love of God. You can find relief in your status as one of His loves, as one of His kids, as one of His "favourites."

• • • • •

Crashing and burning weren't the only unlikely events I was afraid of, over the years. As time went on, I learned about sinkholes. Did you know sometimes the ground literally just opens up and swallows people whole? Of course you know. If you didn't know, please don't google it . . . because I googled it for you.

I'm not making this up. I'm sitting here, re-looking at the CNN article published in 2013. A Floridian guy was, as the article puts it, "entombed" when a massive sinkhole swallowed him into the earth while he slept in his bed. Dude! This stuff happens! I mean, yes, it's pretty rare but, that's real news! This isn't helping, is it? Sorry. Really, I'm sorry.

After sinkholes, I learned about firenadoes, which are exactly what you think they are. Don't YouTube search that word either. Trust me. You're already doing it, aren't you? Please don't. That's not the point of this chapter.

I learned about brown recluse spider bites and terrorist attacks and how rattlesnakes blend into the brush around them, so it's best to avoid all scenarios that involve walking through or near any brush. The likelihood of any of these real and spine-chilling situations happening to us (and ending us) might be small. But the anxious person looks past the statistics and says, "Right, right, right, right, right, but *it happens.* It has happened. It will happen again. To me, specifically. It's happening to me right now, isn't it?"

The anxious person swears off movie theaters because there was a movie theater shooting in Aurora, Colorado. And then when she finally agrees to a chick-flick date night, insists on sitting in the back, so there will be time to escape when the shooter enters through the exit doors down front by the big screen.

Plane crashes and snake venom and men with guns and tornadoes made of fire—these things are real, documented possibilities. And goodness gracious, they *are* scary.

So the anxious person fills his or her life up with fluffier things. Hobby-ish things. Distractions.

As an anxious person myself, I have believed so many surface-level lies that comforted me, and busied myself by feeding tiny identities that, in the quiet, left me feeling empty and shallow.

GOD CAN BE TRUSTED

In a world full of firenadoes, it is so easy to fuel the distracting, temporary, fake identities that help us mask our fears. The problem, of course, is that those identities can't survive the weight of real life. There's not enough substance to any of our Jesus-replacing pursuits. They can't bear up beneath painful realities when they finally break the surface.

There are so many possible examples because options for distractions are everywhere. But pretend you are giving your heart and your time and your focus and your passion to being the greatest make-up artist in the history of rouge. Or pretend you are owned by your hobby as a spinning instructor. You have the "here's how to pedal in just the right way, I think" certification. You have the clip-in shoes that cost more than your car. You have the forty-five-minute spinning mixtape, almost exclusively featuring boy bands, for your class full of sixty-year-old slow peddlers (it's possible this is a personal example). What do you do when the pain you are trying to forget breaks into your life and all you have to comfort yourself with is your art or your spinning or your whatever else it might be?

We weren't meant to have lives built on blush or stationary bikes. If your identity revolves around a job, or a person, or what your body looks like, or anything other than Jesus, you will continue to live burdened; and you will ultimately compound your fear.

If God can't be trusted, natural disasters and venomous creatures and evil people who seek to hurt and kill are enough to send you chasing fake hopes. They are enough to keep you up at night and quadruple-checking your locks and your smoke alarms and your toilet paper rolls (where that one spider lived in Los Angeles when I was five). Lacking control over life, for someone without the Lord, feels like sitting around waiting for whichever catastrophe will strike next. But God always knows what to say.

> "Peace I leave with you. My peace I give to you. I do not give to you as the world gives. Don't let your heart be troubled or fearful." (John 14:27)

> When I am filled with cares, your comfort brings me joy. (Ps. 94:19)

In the midst of this broken world, our God *can* be trusted to give us the perfect gift of His presence. He can be trusted to be with us when we walk through scary things. He can be trusted to be our hope for joy.

He is perfect.

And good.

And loving.

And faithful.

And worthy.

He is our patient, perfect Dad; and He loves us in a way we can't even comprehend, in a way we have never experienced from human to human. He probably looks down at us, us with our plans and our nervous tics and rituals that make us feel better. He looks down at us sitting in our cars practicing over and over the speech we're going to have with our third cousin-in-law twice removed (is that a thing?) who hurt our feelings, as if the phantom conversation will make us feel better.

And God's probably saying, "Come on, kid! What are you *doing*? Why are you so worried? Why are you reciting and panting and crying and counting your breaths and WebMd-ing 'tingly hands' again? All you need to do is rest. Remember My good news? I've already taken care of all the things that keep you up at night . . ."

WORRY IN DISGUISE

I got into my car in a huff the other morning. It was one of the first cold days of the season. My two-year-old had been screaming for a straight, well, probably ten minutes, but it felt like ten hours, and then my oldest proceeded to dump an entire McDonald's cup of ice water all over the backseat. By accident, of course. She's a sweetheart.

I let out a gruff sigh and stomped inside for a towel.

I didn't think I felt scared. I thought I felt annoyed.

You see, my middle child, Joy, who we adopted, goes to a special needs preschool three days a week. She's been going for months, and yet I still haven't figured out how to arrive on schedule without each participant of getting-in-the-car-time having a meltdown.

I wouldn't describe my getting-in-the-car-time frustration as "fear" or "worry," but I knew my feelings needed to be different. I knew I wasn't being joyful or peaceful or loving.

When the mess was wiped up, I plopped down in the front seat and realized the baby wasn't buckled. So, I got back out, slammed my door, opened the back one *again*, and buckled the baby like it was the most challenging chore on Earth.

Again, I knew I needed God's Word. I knew I wasn't being Christlike. I knew I *wanted* to walk gracefully through life's chafing moments with joy, but I wasn't doing it right. So, instead of smiling and patting my sweet tots on the head, I said, "NO TALKING, SCREAMING, CRYING, OR PANICKING. EVERYONE JUST BE QUIET AND LISTEEEEEEEEEN." Then, I pushed "play" on the Bible app and it picked up where it had been playing last. It was Luke 12.

> "I say to you, my friends, don't fear those who kill the body, and after that can do nothing more. But I will show you the one to fear. Fear him who has authority to throw people into hell after death. Yes, I say to you, this is the one to fear! Aren't five sparrows sold for two pennies? Yet not one of them is forgotten in God's sight. Indeed, the hairs of your head are all counted. Don't be afraid; you are worth more than many sparrows." (Luke 12:4–7)

I was losing it and stressing out and talking in all caps to my kids, wondering if I was loved. And God filled my car with supernatural truth and comfort. "Don't be afraid, getting-in-the-car-huffer. You are cared for, door-slammer. You are seen by the One who shaped the world."

When I'm anxious, I start to self-diagnose. And I'm like a child who thinks she's been through medical school because she knows how to use a Band-Aid. I can convince myself I know what my problem is. It's this person. Or it's this possibility. It's definitely this impending danger that's making me feel this way.

But those aren't the things Jesus speaks to. Jesus doesn't address the trifles I'm freaking out over. His Word pierces me. It goes after my heart, right at the root. I'm huffing and puffing and sad and wound up tight, because I'm forgetting that I'm God's. I'm forgetting that the hairs on my head are numbered. Seriously, think about that. Every strand accounted for. I am not "chronically late to special needs preschool mom." I am "more than many sparrows mom." I am "remembered every moment by the Master of it all mom."

If, rather than stumbling in nervously and fixating on my failures, I'm walking in grace and looking upward at the King who has already made me, and remade me and called me His own, I can be known as a woman who is loved by Jesus. And hopefully I can be known as someone who loves like He loves. I'm already worthy because of what Jesus did in my place. I can live in light of Jesus' success rather than the shame of my failures.

In Luke 12, Jesus reminded the disciples how powerful He is. He is powerful over life and death and heaven and hell. And what did He say next? "Don't be afraid." Little children, don't be afraid.

God knew I needed that in my huff. He knew my kids needed it. He knows the world needs it.

I bring this up because I *know* from experience that God's Word is always the answer to your worry problem. Even if you don't realize you have a worry problem. Even if your worry looks more like frustration or sadness or fury-buckling car seats.

God's Word is the answer to the questions you don't even know you have. It's the remedy for fear and selfishness and huffing and puffing.

Not because it's full of beautiful and comforting words, but because it's full of *living* words. It's full of THE Word. Jesus is in that book.

The Bible reminds us who God is. It reminds us who we are. It reminds us Whose we are. It reminds us that we are forgiven. It reminds us that we are rescued. It reminds us that we've already proven we don't have the strength to make it. And it reminds us that God has already proven He'll go to the death to take care of us anyway. And through His Word, the Holy Spirit can comfort us and lead us out of fear and foreboding and back into "the light of the knowledge of God's glory in the face of Jesus Christ" (2 Cor. 4:6).

HOW SELF-RELIANCE FEEDS FEAR

One of the biggest fights Brandon and I ever had was over getting a home security system. Spoiler alert: I'm typing this sentence from my ADT-protected, super secure, fortress of a townhouse. And I've been a proud and loyal customer for over eight years. Victory.

It all started when we lived in a rough neighborhood south of Miami. We paid $600 a month to live in a house owned by the church that employed Brandon. One day I came home from my job at the local Christian school to a string of cop cars with flashing blue lights.

Apparently, our neighbors across the street had been robbed of their, I want to say, forty guns? Maybe fifty? Whatever the number, their too-many guns were removed from their house by some variety of hooligan. Their house that, let me reiterate, was located DIRECTLY ACROSS THE STREET from mine, was broken into and stripped of all its many, many death machines.

I'd just given birth to my first baby. I don't think I need to tell you how exponentially greater anxiety gets when you have a baby. If normal people check to make sure their baby is breathing ten times a night, I mean, you can imagine how many times I checked.

So, back to our fight. I, obviously, insisted that we have an alarm system installed within the hour. And Brandon, my frugal pastor husband, pushed back. I insisted. He declined. I was adamant. He was unmoved. I promised to find a new place to live that was farther from robbers and bullets whether or not he decided to join me. We got the alarm system.

Did I wonder about the criminal history of the ADT installation guy? Sure. Did I immediately change my passcode when he left by calling the ADT headquarters in case he happened to see over my shoulder when I input my alarm code for the first time? That's only for me to know.

I tell you all this to tell you that although I got the alarm system, I still didn't feel safe. Because no alarm company could fix my heart.

There wasn't a moat deep enough, an alarm system loud enough, or a WE HAVE ADT HERE sign big enough to make me feel truly safe.

It is so easy to look at scary situations and believe in something that feels safe in place of trusting the Lord. We can so easily walk away from Jesus and toward this pipe dream, this lie of self-reliance, this idea that we can protect ourself and our people from pain.

If we look inward or look outward, we're going to keep believing the lies. After all, look inward and you'll see your heart, which Jeremiah 17:9 (NIV) says is "deceitful above all things."

If you look outward, you'll see a lot of messages about self-reliance and self-help and safety measures in many forms. Alarm systems, dead bolts, neighborhoods with low crime, twelve-step-programs, gated communities. These things are great and useful, but they can't protect you from life.

They can't prevent disease or disaster or terror from touching your family.

There are brain medicines and counselors that can help you with your fears. There are websites that can teach you how to dig a moat around your home, guys! All these things can help and protect you, *but they won't fix you.* We have got to fight against believing the lies we are told by holding the truth of God's Word up to everything in our minds and everything in front of us. Every day and all the time.

We need to keep God's Word "always on [our] lips" (Josh. 1:8 NIV) and we really do need to "meditate on it day and night" (Ps. 1:2). Because we forget the truth. We forget the Good News that silences the fear.

> Christ Jesus is the one who died, but even more, has been raised; he also is at the right hand of God and intercedes for us. (Rom. 8:34)

God's Word is living and active and it is the only thing that can shift a broken, fearful human brain and transform it into a supernaturally peaceful one.

> For the word of God is living and effective and sharper than any double-edged sword, penetrating as far as the separation of soul and spirit, joints and marrow. It is able to judge the thoughts and intentions of the heart. (Heb. 4:12)

The Bible is not just a book. It is a *living* book. It acts in us as we read it. It remakes us as we remember it.

So how can we do this, practically? I'll help you get started. Here are some of the lies I have struggled with next to the truth of God's Word. If these lies aren't your lies, switch these out for your own, and the alive book God gave us can speak to whatever odd, weirdly specific, tailor-made situation you're obsessing over right now.

Here are some of mine, from years past . . .

> **Lie:** If I lie on the floorboard of the car while Mommy drives through this "bad neighbor-hood," I won't get shot in a drive-by.

> **Truth:** "Even when I go through the darkest valley, I fear no danger, for you are with me; your rod and your staff—they comfort me" (Ps. 23:4).

> **Lie:** If I nag my husband into buying us an ADT alarm system since our neighbors got robbed yesterday, we will be safe from criminal invasion.

> **Truth:** "One who is righteous has many adversities, but the LORD rescues him from them all" (Ps. 34:19).

> **Lie:** If I can completely avoid sleep during my firstborn baby's first year of life, I can monitor her breathing 24/7 and ensure that she doesn't die from SIDS; and then once she turns one, I can get a solid eight hours. (By the way, sorry, but this doesn't exist. A solid eight hours never happens again. Never.)

Truth: "We are afflicted in every way but not crushed; we are perplexed but not in despair; we are persecuted but not abandoned; we are struck down but not destroyed" (2 Cor. 4:8–9).

It's interesting what God's Word promises about His protection. It doesn't sound anything like the security system ads. Those ads tell you they can keep you from being the victim of a crime.

God's Word doesn't promise an escape or a life free from trouble. In fact, His Word actually promises the opposite.

In John 16:33, Jesus said, "I have told you these things so that in me you may have peace. You will have suffering in this world. Be courageous! I have conquered the world." God doesn't promise us easy; He promises us victory.

Peace does not come from having enough protective measures. I know it because I've lived it. I tried with all my might to insulate myself and my people from every danger that caught my radar. But I wasn't peaceful, because I wasn't just running from fear, I was running from God. I was hiding from the problem and the Answer.

I was literally barricading myself from the Prince of Peace.

God said, "You will be hated by everyone because of my name" (Matt. 10:22), but I didn't want to be hated.

God said I would have suffering in this world. But some people suffer less than others, right? Maybe I could be like more of a Kate Middleton, Duchess of Cambridge, and less like a long-suffering Job.

AFRAID OF A BOOK

It's weird to be afraid of a book. It is even weirder to be afraid of only parts of a book. But I spent so many years running from the one thing that would give me what I was looking for because I only focused on the parts I didn't like. I didn't like pain. I wanted to avoid suffering. That was my main mission and I thought that was okay. I can't tell you how many times I have identified myself as "daughter of a SWAT cop" with a little shrug, like "I can't help it; this is just my lot in life . . . I'm a paranoid person. I don't love it, but that's just what I am . . ."

My thoughts revolved so much around my fears, and my choices were so centered around avoiding them, that fear was built into my very identity. My fears were what defined me.

"I'm an anxious person, so . . ."

"Well, I was raised by a police officer, so . . ."

"I mean, my mom got held up with a gun and my grandma was mugged that time. And yeah, nothing good happens after midnight. I'm just a realist is all . . ."

Anxious person. Cop's daughter. Seasoned realist who knows the true nature of the world. Practical exceptor of sinkholes.

Throughout my life, I'd catch little glimpses of people with peace. But my cynicism was louder than their witness.

I'd think, *Well, that person seems to be settled in the Lord, but they've got to have a crutch. They're hiding something.*

Cynic.

It was all laid out for me in God's Word, the remedy, but I didn't want to see it. I only saw the malady. I wanted the Good Book to say, "Follow Me, and nothing bad will happen to you."

I wanted it to say, "You can be the 'cop's daughter,' and I'll be your new and improved bodyguard if you just follow Me."

But instead, God told me that following Him would make people hate me. He said that following Him would be difficult. He said that I would walk through the darkest valleys.

That was enough to make me scared and make me run.

Until He helped me see that wasn't all He said. He said it would be difficult. He said it would be dark. But the book I was afraid of also included something else He said: that He would be with me.

And then He showed me that was more than enough.

• • • • •

On the website Desiring God, John Piper says, "Jesus loves to free his people from their anxieties and fears. He exalts his power and superiority by working to take away what troubles us. Anxiety stems from a *lack of faith* in our heavenly Father, as unbelief gets the upper hand in our hearts. Much anxiety, Jesus says, comes from little faith."[3]

We anxiety-prone people don't want to hear that sometimes our fear reveals that we have a faith problem, a belief problem, a trusting God problem. That's the *most* scary thing.

We don't want to camp out in the discomfort of sanctification, because if we don't breathe deeply of the grace of God in those moments our sin is exposed, we will fall into self-loathing. God certainly doesn't want us there. Instead, He wants our focus off of self and on Him. That's what humility is.

Rick Warren put it this way, "Humility is not thinking less of yourself; it is thinking of yourself less."[4]

We shouldn't think of our sin OR our successes. Our questions should be *Who does God say that I am? What does God say I'm worth? What have I done to deserve His great love?*

And every one of those questions takes us right to the cross. And as we stand in its shadow, we remember why we're here. The cross says I am broken AND loved. The cross says God considered saving me a thing worth the death of His Son. The cross says I've done nothing to deserve the great love of God, but Jesus did everything and I get it for free.

We remember that every breath we're given is another moment of opportunity—opportunity to enjoy the love of Christ. It is another chance to share the love of Christ with a world that's passing away—a world that is lost with even more reason to be scared than you are. To the lost, death stings. To those without Christ, death is the end. But us? We have Him. We have life. We have hope.

A FOURTEEN-HOUR FLIGHT FROM NEW JERSEY TO BEIJING

Back in March of this year, I did the most airplane flying I'd ever done as my brood ventured to China and back to adopt our little Joy.

I'll tell you more about Joy's miraculous story in later chapters, but when we first saw her picture, she was an almost four-year-old with no ears. She couldn't hear, couldn't walk, and couldn't communicate in any way. And somehow God got our attention and led us down a path to pick up and bring home this little miracle, who is now a chubby, walking, hearing (with a hearing aid), American Sign Language learning, happy little joy to our whole family. Sweet Joy.

We didn't know that's how Joy's story would turn out. We just knew God wanted us to go get her. So we boarded that fourteen-hour flight headed toward that little girl whose medical file gave our pediatrician "great hesitation." And we buckled our one-year-old and five-year-old into their first airplane seats and flew right over the North Pole. Seriously.

That reads pretty scary typed out like that. So it seems all the more amazing that we sipped on our tomato juice (I only drink tomato juice on airplanes) with hearts full of peace.

We flew from Nashville to New Jersey to Beijing (that leg of it is the fourteen-hour flight). Then we took a bullet train to Tianjin, picked up Joy from the orphanage, flew to Guangzhou, drove to Hong Kong, flew to San Francisco, and then finally flew back to Nashville.

So as we were gearing up to get on those planes and break the mold of our monotonous, comfortable, predictable little life-rhythms of Franklin, Tennessee, we were having some conversations too close to our kids, and the ears of my then-five-year-old happened to turn on. She caught a snippet of sarcastic conversation that was intended to stay between adults.

Brandon and I were discussing flight routes and mostly joking as we debated whether we'd rather crash and burn over the North Pole or Russia. She may have also caught the tidbit about how I saw thirty seconds of some Netflix show where the intro showed a plane crash and people's faces melting off.

"Mommy?" Ever said, approaching me from out of thin air (she always does this when I'm having conversations I think/hope she's not hearing), "I don't think I want to go to China anymore to get Joy . . . I don't want to die in a plane crash. And I don't want my face to melt."

And I looked at her and decided right then to tell her about Jesus and the sweet truth instead of airplane springs and a sweet lie.

I told her that planes crash. And sometimes people die in plane crashes. But hardly ever. I told her I didn't know enough about the human body or thermodynamics (is it thermodynamics?) to know if faces melt in that sort of situation. I told her (unsure as I said it, whether it was a good idea to keep going) that a few years ago a man in Florida died in his bed because a sinkhole opened up under his house. I told her that meteors have fallen from outer space. And that people die in car crashes, even when they are making good driving choices.

Then I told her that God, who loves us so much, is in total control of everything.

I told her that if God wants Mommy or Daddy or her or anyone else in heaven, it doesn't matter if they are on a plane or in their bed or watching TV or in China. I told her that Jesus is the only One who has power over life and death. I told her that, what is even more amazing, is that He defeated death on the cross. He walked out of His own grave. I told her that if He has work for our family on Earth, He is strong enough to keep that plane in the air and protect us.

I reminded her that He *so* loves her.

And as the words rolled off my tongue, the Holy Spirit reminded me too.

I told her that bad things happen in this broken world, but that Jesus has overcome the world (John 16:33). I told her that for followers of Jesus, "to live is Christ and to die is gain" (Phil. 1:21).

I said these things, fully expecting them to not help or fly over her head or maybe even make things worse.

But the Holy Spirit took His Words, and cast out my little then-five-year-old's fear of flying with His perfect love (1 John 4:18). With His very own Word. Just like that.

"Oh! Okay," she chirped, "I still want to go to China, then."

And we did. We flew to China and we flew back.

The sweet truth trumps any sweet lie we can come up with, on the fly.

I didn't want to crash over the North Pole or Russia. I didn't want to have a melty face, but those weeks leading up to our flight, I knew that I didn't have to be afraid. God has proven to me so many times that He is real, that He really loves me, that He is in control, and that I can trust Him.

A REAL PLANE CRASH

My friend, Kelly, was in an actual plane crash.

I met Kelly during a weird phase of my life when I felt unlovable and undeserving, and I had a short punk haircut with a bleached stripe that I dyed bright red. Kelly was my mom's age and she was kind to me.

It was weird. Because I was weird, and Kelly showed me no judgment. She took the time to talk to me and get to know me. She was gracious and encouraging and loving.

And strong and brave and witty.

And also a plane crash survivor.

Kelly has obviously been interviewed a bajillion times about her unfathomable experience. In 2012, the *Washington Post* quoted her as she explained how she felt during the aftermath of the crash: "I was kind of afraid of God at that point. I thought He must be really mad at me."

Kelly was a flight attendant for Air Florida. On January 13, 1982, Flight 90 hit a bridge and crashed into the Potomac River. She was one of only five survivors. I don't know the exact time line of her testimony, but I know that surviving a plane crash was a pivotal moment. I know that what started out as fear and "God must be really mad at me" turned to faith in "God really loves me."

I know this because I've known Kelly for years. She is one of the easiest laughers I've ever met. She's truly funny and over-the-top kind and strikingly genuine and supernaturally calm. And she just lost an adult child to a car accident last year. And can I remind you, she's been in a plane crash? And yet, she's still Kelly. She's still a woman who loves God so much that peace and joy and laughter spill out of her.

Whether she's happy or grieving or giggling or mourning, Kelly overflows with a love and a groundedness that, after all she's been through, can only be explained as a miracle of God. A peace that surpasses all understanding.

> And the peace of God, which surpasses all understanding, will guard your hearts and minds in Christ Jesus. (Phil. 4:7)

See, we're all going to suffer through scary situations. We all have and we all will again. But we can suffer differently than the rest of the world suffers. We can cry and scream and wrestle through the deep pains of life like people who know that hope is just up ahead. When we remember how soon scary things will cease, we no longer have to be false-happy or wallowing in circumstance.

> Yet you do not know what tomorrow will bring—what your life will be! For you are like a vapor that appears for a little while, then vanishes. (James 4:14)

What a happy reality for us. The sad and the scary is only for a little while . . .

> Then I saw a new heaven and a new earth; for the first heaven and the first earth had passed away, and the sea was no more. I also saw the holy city, the new Jerusalem, coming down out of heaven from God, prepared like a bride adorned for her husband. Then I heard a loud voice from the throne: Look, God's dwelling is with humanity, and he will live with them. They will be his peoples, and God himself will be with them and will be their God. He will wipe away every tear from their eyes. Death will be no more; grief, crying, and pain will be no more, because the previous things have passed away. Then the one seated on the throne said, "Look, I am making everything new." He also said, "Write, because these words are faithful and true." Then he said to me, "It is done! I am the Alpha and the

Omega, the beginning and the end. I will freely give to the thirsty from the spring of the water of life. The one who conquers will inherit these things, and I will be his God, and he will be my son." (Rev. 21:1–7)

• • • • •

Last year, I read *The Lion, the Witch, and the Wardrobe* to my oldest. One of my favorite parts of the book is when Mr. Beaver, one of the characters, is talking about Aslan. The book was written by C. S. Lewis, and although it involves talking beavers and ice queens, it is actually a giant gospel allegory. So Aslan is this huge, majestic lion that represents Jesus. He's kind and frightening and wonderful. And in the book, Mr. Beaver is talking to Lucy, a little girl, about him.

> Lucy asks Mr. Beaver if Aslan is "safe."
> "Safe?" said Mr. Beaver; "don't you hear what Mrs. Beaver tells you? Who said anything about safe? 'Course he isn't safe. But he's good. He's the King, I tell you."[5]

Jesus isn't safe. But who said anything about safe?

Praise be to God, I can smile as I type that now. Because I'm no longer defined by my fears. I no longer run to lies for comfort. I run to His Word. Because while He's not safe, He's *so* good. And "he's the King, I tell you."

Chapter Three

GOD, PLEASE DON'T MAKE ME MOVE TO AFRICA

• •• •• • • • •• •• •• •

I've never actually asked God not to move me to Africa. I mean, I thought about it. I wanted to ask. I probably even started to, but then I thought it better to pretend I never had the thought in the first place.

I have often been afraid that the voodoo-like quality I'd ascribed to God would activate and He would either make my husband move me to a place that gives you automatic leprosy, or He'd haunt me with guilt and make me feel like a "backslider" for not "answering the call" for the rest of my life.

I spent many of my Christ-seeking years half-in, putting Christian-ese phrases such as "answering the call" in quotation marks, and the root of that cynicism has most always been fear. I was afraid that in God's supernatural kingdom, surrender would only and always mean suffering.

I was afraid of what "answering a call" might look like. So I threw up air quotes in my heart and tried not to think about how easy it was for me to neglect the God I claimed to adore.

I thought things like, *If I really allow myself to be close to God, He's going to test me tomorrow with full-on boils. If I really press in, God will immediately demand I move to a third-world country and then there I will contract the Staph infection that will end me.*

I know it sounds crazy, but if you're reading this, maybe you understand. A mind ruled by anxiety kind of *is* crazy. And minds like that are everywhere. You find yourself thinking and worrying about obscure things that don't seem to cross the minds of people around you, and you wonder, *Where did that even come from?*

Just the other night a friend of mine texted me for "how to start writing professionally" advice and then went on to say that she was stressed out that a lot of people might begin reading the articles she hadn't started writing yet and then maybe her weird friend from high school may find the articles and want to be her weird friend again. After she shared that I thought, *Is it weird that I don't think that is weird? In fact, which of my weird high school friends is about to find me right this second? I should ask all the publications that have posted my articles to delete them and then maybe change my name and move.*

Maybe you can relate. Maybe, like me, you look at the actual words of the Bible, and you try to read them, but somehow you find yourself believing the enemy as he twists Scripture.

In the past, I'd read verses like these:

> "If anyone comes to Me, and does not hate his own father and mother, wife and children, brothers and sisters—yes, even his own life—he cannot be my disciple." (Luke 14:26)

> "In the same way, therefore, every one of you who does not renounce all his possessions cannot be my disciple." (Luke 14:33)

> In fact, all who want to live a godly life in Christ Jesus will be persecuted. (2 Tim. 3:12)

And I'd take those verses to mean that unless I was hating life and completely miserable, I was failing as a Christian.

Yeah! Sign me up! Persecution! Yes please! Comfort? No way. Those Chobani Flip yogurts I love? Almond Coco Loco? May they be from me as far as the east is from the west. Holy people eat almost expired bread and give all the Coco Loco to the homeless.

And hatred from the people closest to me, do I want that? Obviously! How quickly can that kick in?

During the years I wrestled with the fear of a hard life for Jesus, I had tasted and seen that He is good already. But

I spent so many of my days, so much of my brain power, on keeping relational harmony with my family members, on acquiring the things I needed and wanted, on trying to be safe, that I rarely took the time to taste. There was always looming tragedy to avoid that kept my attention from Christ. It felt like my whole life was contradicting what I said I believed.

I was so afraid to speak it out loud or even think it—the underlying truth that I wanted the comforts of this world more than I wanted the Comforter.

Because I believed in Jesus and I believed that His Word was true, I was certain that as soon as I let my guard down, God would wreck my life. I thought God would take away everything I loved. That He would send me to a foreign land to be executed by people who hate His Name.

I read about happy martyrs like they were aliens. Have you heard of Hugh Latimer, the English pastor who was burned at a stake in the 1500s? As he was preparing to burn next to his friend, it is told that he said, "Be of good comfort, Master Ridley, and play the man; we shall this day light such a candle, by God's grace, in England, as I trust shall never be put out."[6] Just, how? How? I couldn't understand how people could face terror with joy and peace and the fact that it was such a foreign concept to me was the scariest thing of all. I was constantly questioning my salvation.

I'd read so much about God, and I'd talked at Him for so many years. But, often, I skimmed over His Word rather than interacting with Him in it. I focused my energies on chick-flick viewing and dream dates and creative projects. Anything that would take my mind off of eternity and all the ways I was failing in light of eternity. I was scared that, heaven forbid, I was doing it all wrong.

And when I did take a two-minute sliver out of my day to look at the words of Jesus, I usually thought, *I believe that this is true . . . but, God sounds very hard to please.*

I believed God was who He said He was, but I didn't have the courage to get to know Him. I didn't know who I was in Him.

AFRAID OF MISSIONS PEOPLE

I used to feel very uncomfortable around "missions" people. You know who I'm talking about. The people who move to third-world countries on purpose or who run mission teams at church or people who try to get you to think about going on missions trips. I avoided these people because I assumed that they'd either pressure me to do something I didn't want to do, or they'd take one look at me and label me a bad Christian for not wanting to be a part of their particular missional interest. My fear was so thick that I subconsciously avoided listening to God.

About five years ago, our friends Jake and Anna were visiting and Anna said something that stuck with me. I was sharing some of these Africa/leprosy/boil/missionary-related fears with her.

She said, "Shame and worry are not from God. You're His daughter. If He wants you to move to Africa, you're going to *want to* move to Africa. God loves you, Scarlet. Wherever He leads you, He's going to give you joy in it . . ."

King David thought the same thing. He wrestled lions and battled giants, which, on the surface, seems harder than moving to another country and he said in Psalm 37:4 (ESV), "Delight yourself in the LORD, and he will give you the desires of your heart."

I don't know why I've always had the idea that living for God meant kicking and screaming my way through a miserable life. Paul wasn't miserable as he was stoned and beaten for God. I'm sure it wasn't his favorite, but he counted it all as joy.

After Jake and Anna left, I stood in the kitchen of my little apartment and said, "God . . . I'm scared to talk to You . . . I'm scared to want You . . ."

Everything in me wanted to end my prayer there. Everything in me wanted to look at my phone and get affirmation from strangers on Facebook. Everything in me wanted to shout upstairs, "Ever, let's go to the park!" But I forced myself to stand still. I forced myself to feel the fear and look to God.

I continued, now through tears, "God, I don't want to be close to You, because I know that as soon as I am, You're going to take my daughter. You're going to test me. You're going to take Brandon away. Right?"

And the Holy Spirit responded with gentleness. He responded with His Word. He responded with "The Cure for Anxiety" as my Bible's subheading calls it.

"Therefore I tell you: Don't worry about your life, what you will eat or what you will drink: or about your body, what you will wear. Isn't life more than food and the body more than clothing? Consider the birds of the sky: They don't sow or reap or gather into barns, yet your heavenly Father feeds them. Aren't you worth more than they?" (Matt. 6:25–26)

Well, I guess I'm worth more to You than the birds, but look at Job. He loved you and You let Satan take everything he loved . . .

I read again . . . "If you then, who are evil, know how to give good gifts to your children, how much more will your Father in heaven give good things to those who ask him" (Matt. 7:11).

It's hard to explain the big meaningful interactions I've had with God. They tend to have a major you-had-to-be-there feel. But as I stood in that kitchen, enveloped in the agony of my fear, I felt God reach in and brush it away effortlessly, like when you gently blow a stray hair out of your face and back into place. In that little, weirdly shaped kitchen, God poured the truth of His Word into my soul. In those minutes that I didn't run from His presence, the words I'd read and known and twisted into condemnation were clear. "How much more will your Father in heaven give good things?"

I stood in that kitchen and cried in His arms. I can't remember what my then-three-year-old was doing up in her room, but I was standing on holy kitchen linoleum as the Lord reassured me, that I am loved, not because I am good, but because He is good. I am scared, but He is good.

> The LORD is good to everyone; his compassion rests on all he has made. (Ps. 145:9)

> Every good and perfect gift is from above, coming down from the Father of lights, who does not change like shifting shadows. (James 1:17)

God doesn't delight in hurting His children. His wrath is not poured out on His beloved. When He looks out at His broken people living in this still-so-broken world, He is full of mercy and compassion. And when we walk through the pains of death and trauma and our crippling imaginary concerns, He isn't the enemy. He isn't the aggressor. He's the Comforter.

> Blessed be the God and Father of our Lord Jesus Christ, the Father of mercies and the God of all comfort. He comforts us in all our affliction, so that we may be able to comfort those who are in any kind of affliction, through the comfort we ourselves receive from God. For just as the sufferings

of Christ overflow to us, so also through
Christ our comfort overflows. (2 Cor. 1:3–5)

When the Holy Spirit gave me the grace to see God as
my Good Father and Comforter in this world broken by
sin, I stopped running away from Him and started running to Him. When the gospel made clear that God has
already given me His own Son, I stopped being afraid of
the "scary" situations that bring me close to Him.

LOOKING FOR JOY INSTEAD OF FEAR

These days, instead of looking to avoid missions that
might make me miserable, I look for missions that move me
with joy. It's pretty amazing. Being freed from the fear of
serving God has given me actual joy and real peace about
opportunities that most people (including me) would consider "scary."

The reality that in God's kingdom, joy can come even
with discomfort and even during pain has finally clicked
for me. Not everyone is supposed to go to Africa. You don't
have to have leprosy. But all Christians are called to live out
the Great Commission in whatever way and in whichever
place God leads them. Not every Christian will experience
the pain of their biggest fear, but all Christians will walk
through pain. But they will walk through it with Jesus.

I could have so easily shrouded my life with joy-stealing
distractions forever, because I'm a coward. But thankfully,
God gave me the grace to lower my defensive stance just

long enough to hear His voice and be comforted by His goodness and His Good News. And that comfort allowed me to find a mission.

It wasn't Africa, but China—a communist country where you're not allowed to talk about Jesus. So far, no boils.

God gave me actual joy and real-life peace as I input our personal information onto the United Airlines' website selecting seats for a flight that would take me, my husband, and my two daughters (Brooklyn, the one we call Dewy, was only one-year-old when we got on that plane) to this foreign land to bring home a new family member, who, at almost four years old, wasn't walking or communicating in any way. God gave me a desire that sounded scary. He made me want it. And He gave me the courage to do it. And the blessings He's given us through it all have been immeasurable.

FINDING JOY IN PERSONAL CALLINGS

A few Mondays ago, I was sitting on a barstool in the living room of a family that used their frequent flyer miles to send my family to China and back. Our small group was meeting at their house that day, and we were discussing Romans 12, where Paul talks about the body of Christ—how we all play a different role and how we all have different functions.

> Now as we have many parts in one body, and all the parts do not have the same function, in the same way we who are many are one body in Christ and individually members of one another. According to the grace given to us, we have different gifts: If prophesy, use it according to the proportion of one's faith; if service, use it in service; if teaching, in teaching; if exhorting, in extortion; giving, with generosity; leading, with diligence; showing mercy, with cheerfulness. (Rom. 12:4–8)

So, we read those verses together. And the coolest thing happened.

We went around the circle talking about the desires and the more uncomfortable callings the Lord had given each of us. And it was shocking how different our dreams were.

One family in the circle said they wanted to foster middle school boys. WHAT! Another said they wanted to get involved in children's ministry at church. My husband laughed and said, "This is so crazy! I definitely don't want to foster middle school boys, and the Lord would have to speak audibly from the throne room of heaven for me to serve in children's ministry, but I really wanted to adopt a deaf girl with no ears!"

And we all laughed and had a moment of happy disbelief. God is right and His Word is true, and we were seeing it in the strange hopes of the people we love. God gives us different desires and different gifts and different places of the world or town or church to serve in; and when we're seeking His will, He gives us joy in it. How cool.

AFRAID OF UNREACHED PEOPLE

Brandon and I were on a date the other night, about a week ago, and we were sitting outside in perfect weather, mid-70s, sipping coffee with fancy whipped cream on top, and he said, "I hope the Lord gives us the desire, someday in our lives, maybe when the girls are grown, to spend the rest of our years bringing the gospel to unreached people groups."

As He "dropped this bomb" as I called it in the moment, our Chinese-American daughter, only six months home at the time, was being put to bed by a sweet teenage girl from our church. The moment he said this was almost precisely the moment I'd moved from survival-mode to sort-of-comfortable-mode. So my knee-jerk reaction was anger.

Yes. I'm super godly. So very holy.

When we adopted Joy and she still couldn't walk or communicate, we spent so much time making medical appointments and going to specialists and parenting through the emotionally tumultuous aftermath of her traumatic first three and a half years of neglect. And now here we were. She was walking. She was communicating. And miracle of miracles, she was being put to bed by a teenage babysitter. And we were sipping fancy coffee in our beautiful neighborhood Starbucks, and Brandon mentions moving to a third-world country.

I'm so thankful I married this man. This man who knows the heart of God and knows how loved he is so much that his dreams don't involve better cars and bigger homes and larger grocery budgets. His dreams revolve around the kingdom of heaven, that, someday, won't have sinkholes or cancer or terrorism.

I'm thankful. But, sometimes, when I'm more focused on this temporal kingdom that is passing away, sometimes, when my eyes aren't looking up like they should be, kingdom-talk catches me off guard. And my knee-jerk response is old-me. My initial reaction is to cling to my whipped creams.

We had a miniature squabble at the neighborhood Starbucks that night as I acted like a spoiled child, and he reiterated with a calm smile, "I'm not saying let's go! I'm not even saying that I want to. I'm saying that *I want to want that* someday."

When we got home, Brandon sat in his chair and read page ten-thousand-million from his dragon book (he likes fantasy fiction, but it's okay, he's obviously got other great qualities) and I went upstairs, opened my computer, and searched YouTube for "unreached people groups."

As I watched YouTube videos, I thought about my little Joy. Joy, who, in most every photo we have of her in China, had a red Buddhist dot painted on her forehead. Bubbly, silly, gentle-natured Joy who might never have heard the good news of Jesus and the lasting joy He brings, had we not gone to get her and bring her home. As I researched unreached people groups from my fluffy, white bed, I could hear my little, formerly-unreached, heavy-breathing Joy from a room away, as she was getting over a cold. And I thought about what matters most and the joy and peace that have come from the gospel-fueled trust that lets me ask God to replace my desires with His.

We may never travel overseas again. Or, maybe we will. But if we do, we'll want to, because when we ask God to break our hearts for what breaks His, and when we mean it, and when we do it with hearts that see more cross than fear and more Christ than doubt, He answers. He gives us the desires of our hearts, His desires, and He showers us with blessings in the midst of it.

WHEN THE UNREACHED PEOPLE ARE RIGHT NEXT DOOR

A few years ago, I met someone in my neighborhood while I was out getting the mail or something. She was friendly and had a couple kids with her and invited us to go to the park. We went, and listen, I live in the Bible Belt now, so it's not at all uncommon to meet Christians. In fact, I'm working on this chapter in a Whole Foods right now, and I'm in a booth next to two college-aged girls, and the song I was listening to just ended and here was the snippet of conversation I picked up from that booth: "If I just accept the grace of Jesus and realize that I need Him, that I'm a sinner who can't save myself, that I can't earn His love, I can rest in that . . ." I truly almost got up, amen-ed, gave her a hug and started a slow clap. Anyway, that's where I live! And that's not an abnormal occurrence.

Also, just on a personal note, it's hard for me to get to know people without Jesus naturally coming up because He is part of mine and my husband's professions. My husband's job titles, over the years, have included Campus Pastor, Worship Leader, Sunday School Curriculum Strategist (something like that), and now Bible Study Marketer (again, *something* like that) and of course, I write about Jesus. Those are our jobs, so Jesus pretty much comes up, right out of the gate.

So, I go to the park with this lady. Our kids are running around swinging and sliding and smashing into each other, and because this woman is responding to my Jesus-talk with similar sounding lingo, I'm blabbering on, like I'm talking to a sister. She told me the name of her church, and once I got home, I realized she and her family were actually part of a very well-known cult in the area.

Noooooooooooooo!

When I learned this, I got scared. I got distant. I with-drew and got busy. And a year went by, and then she moved away. And I felt so much shame. I felt so much guilt. God put a lost person right in my neighborhood. God allowed me to have access to her and her kids. She wanted to go to the park with us! And I was closed off.

I actually felt the guilt before I knew they were moving. Somewhere in there, I decided maybe I could start a Bible study in my neighborhood and invite a few others and her, and maybe then I'd have a second chance to share the gospel with her. But, by the time I got over my fear of interacting with her, she was so involved in her cult's activities, she didn't have a single free day of the week. She spent every single day at that building.

I talked to my sister one night and told her how ashamed I was. How scared I'd been. How guilty I felt.

And my sweet Aubrey, eight years my junior, my little baby biscuit, spoke this truth over me. She said, "Pickles (that's what she calls me), if God is going to save that family, your sin is not going to stop Him in His pursuit. Your fear is not going to keep them from finding the real Jesus. You have missed out on the blessing of being used by God in their lives because of your fear, but you can't believe the lie that anything you did or didn't do had the power to hijack their salvation."

I was telling my seven-year-old the other day how to know if she was hearing from God. I told her, if you think God is telling you something, hold that something up to Scripture. In John 1, Jesus is called "the Word." If the words in your head don't mesh with His words, then they're not from Him.

So, I held Aubrey's word up to the Word.

> For he tells Moses, I will show mercy to whom I will show mercy, and I will have compassion on whom I will have compassion. So then, it does not depend on human will or effort but on God who shows mercy. (Rom. 9:15–16)

God is the one who saves. Nothing can help Him save and nothing can stop Him from saving. Not my best efforts at starting a guilt-infused, belated, cult-clearing Bible study and not my sin and fear that caused me to fail in the first place. I repented of my disobedience, but then I get to rest again in the obedience of Christ.

God's love for me is based on His good work, not mine. God is the one who shows mercy.

That's the truth. That's not just a Band-Aid that helps me sleep at night. I'm so prone, SO CRAZY PRONE to fall back into my old ways of thinking—to forget that Jesus does good and I'm merely a servant of His. Maybe you are too. We can say, "Yes Lord!" or "Here I am, send me! (Isa. 6:8) and experience the wonder of being a tool in His hands, or we can cower in fear and hide in a corner and watch opportunities to love and serve Him and His people pass us by. Does God use us to lead people to Himself? YES. Does God *need us* to save people? NO.

Thank God, we can walk through this life without shame and regret. Jesus loves you, though you fail. And Jesus saves people, though you let opportunities to share His love slip through your fingers sometimes.

If you are afraid of loving someone, don't be. God will bless you with joy as you reach out of your comfort zone to lead lost people to hope. If you are full of remorse for with-holding love in your fear, accept God's forgiveness and turn from it. Next time, as the Spirit burdens you for a family, or a friend, or a stranger, let them into your life and share what God has already done through Jesus.

There will be times you will be rejected and you will need to "shake the dust off your feet" (Matt. 10:14), but other times, you'll get to witness the miracle of salvation. You'll get to be there when someone experiences the love and peace that only Jesus can give a lost, restless, and anxious soul. It is the coolest thing.

There is nothing I've experienced in my life that has been more stunning than seeing God change people through the power of His Word. We get to be part of it, and we don't have to be afraid of other countries or bad neighborhoods or cult members or communist governments, because our God is more powerful than the evil we see on Earth. He's already proven that by crushing evil at the cross, and through the cross He has already given that power to us.

JONAH DIDN'T LIKE BAD NEIGHBORHOODS EITHER

Miami is a unique place in that the pockets of violent crime are just a brisk walk from the beachside mansions. You could live in the nicest gated community in South Florida, but if you go one block the wrong direction while walking your dog, you will probably become the victim of a kidnapping. That's what I thought, anyway. It felt intense. My dad saw it all, every night, and wanted to protect us, so he told us what was out there. And he has half a pinky, shot off during a SWAT drug bust, to prove it.

So when I lived in Miami, I didn't want to drive through or even near bad neighborhoods, let alone actually GO

INTO THEM. I remember being in the car with my mom and seeing her tense up as she said, pre-GPS of course, "Uh . . . we're lost . . . and this is . . . a . . . bad neighborhood."

My massive fear of bad guys overpowered my medium fear of not wearing a seat belt, so I'd unbuckle and literally slide down to the floorboard. The thought process was *If someone starts shooting, but I'm one with the floormat, I'll be fine.*

When I reflect back on how fear used to define me and inform my decisions, I identify so much with Jonah. God told him to get up and go to a scary town. An evil city. Essentially, a "bad neighborhood."

In verse 2 of the book, we see God say, "Get up! Go to the great city of Nineveh and preach against it because their evil has come up before me" (Jonah 1:2).

Go to the evil place? The danger zone? Where the bad guys live? You want me to walk into that? And preach *against* it?

Jonah said no.

But trouble found him anyway. He got stuck on a boat in a storm. He got oh-my-gosh-how-can-this-be-happening-for-real-right-now swallowed by a fish big enough to make that happen. God, in His grace, was showing him, "Hey . . . um . . . I'm literally in control of the universe. I can create a fish big enough to swallow you and then make him do it and you're worried about obeying Me?"

And Jonah prayed from inside the belly of the whale. And the whale spat Jonah out on dry land. A second chance. A very messy and unconventional second chance, but still a second chance.

Go read the book of Jonah. It's such a great book. After God redirected Jonah in such a gracious and creative way, Jonah got a one-way ticket to Nineveh and witnessed to the people there. He experienced the love and mercy of God and couldn't wait to tell all the "scary" Ninevites about it. And in chapter 3, we see the people of Nineveh turn to God. Heart change. And God used Jonah to do it.

Why did Jonah change? Why did he go to Nineveh? Because he witnessed God's power. God's protection. God's mercy. He experienced God. Even in his disobedience. Even as he ran from God, God pursued him.

He went boldly into the bad neighborhood when he started trusting God.

THE HOLY SPIRIT CAN MAKE YOU BRAVE TOO

I have a vivid memory of being thirteen, standing in front of the bathroom mirror with the door locked, repeatedly shout-singing "It's All Coming Back to Me Now" by Celine Dion as tears streamed down my face.

I wasn't in love with anyone.

In fact, I didn't really know anyone.

We had just moved back to Los Angeles, from Miami, and the only people I knew or saw, ever, were my sister, Aubrey, who was five at the time, my mom, and our landlord, who gave us such intense heebie-jeebies that we would literally drop to floor and crawl into the other room to hide when we saw her puttering around in the courtyard from the front window.

Though my love interests were nonexistent, I was completely overwhelmed by just the possibility of being in love. I was so overcome with imaginary passion that I could cry just saying the words, "I love you" to some mystery man who, at the time, was a strange blend of Tom Everett Scott, the actor who played the drummer who wore sunglasses from *That Thing You Do!*, Dimitri, the love interest in Anastasia, and Zac, the youngest Hanson brother.

I was obsessed with the idea that I could feel so intensely about a person. And that someone could love me back.

The point is, now I'm an old married lady with a few kids. By the time you read this, I'll have been married TWELVE years. Goodness. And, though we *are* passionately in love, we don't stand in the living room and sob as we sing romantic ballads to each other. Most days we stand in the kitchen while our little girls sob and we make trying-not-to-laugh faces at each other. My fantasy at thirteen didn't quite line up with the reality of romantic love.

But even though those longings I had for earth-shattering romance may have been more intense than they needed to be, I think I was on the nose when it comes to the love between God and His kids.

Let me tell you about a cool thing that happened to me at church.

I'm part of this church that I love. A few years ago, we moved out of a warehouse and into a new church building.

So, energy was high and a lot of us entered the building with teary excitement, as of course, getting into this place was a group effort that we got to be a part of in a bunch of ways.

So, before anyone even came up to the pulpit, we got to watch a video. Oh man, this video. It started in Genesis and went through the history of the spread of Christianity. Stephen being stoned. The spread of the gospel to Ethiopia. China. The West. The founding of the Nashville Baptist Association. The church that planted us. Our warehouse building. And then the final picture was of the building we were sitting in for the first time. It was so incredible to watch. I could hear the collective sniffling and what I felt was something rare. That intensity. That extra rare Celine-Dion-level church intensity.

As the video faded to black, I thought about Christians who live in countries where they are being beheaded for owning pages of the Bible or meeting together to worship God. Then, I had a thought I've had before. What if a gunman came in here right now?

Obviously, I've spent many a day playing out (obsessing over) worst-case-scenarios. My church-gunman exit strategy would usually go something like . . . *Where are the exits? If the terrorist walked in, how would I get to my girls if he was standing between me and their rooms? If I manage to get my people and get out but then the car on my right swerves into my lane, is the left lane empty? Also, are there any tornadoes forming within a one-hundred-mile radius of me, as I flee the gunman carrying my children (one under each arm and the tiniest one wrapped around my neck like a scarf)? And just double-checking, Tennessee is, after all, a top five state for sinkholes, right? (It is.)*

But, on this particular Sunday, my thought pattern was simpler. I thought to myself, *If a gunman walked in right now, I think I could face death with joy.*

That sounds crazy! Even as I thought that thought, I was startled. I wasn't plagued by my normal exit strategy reel. My primary feeling was oddly similar to the feeling I had standing in front of the mirror as a thirteen-year-old girl. I felt a complete and passionate love for Someone. Love that would say, "Yes, I belong to God. If you kill me for it, it's totally worth it."

Love that overpowers fear.

I love when God gives me the grace to see life that way.

At thirteen, the lyrics in my heart were, "There were moments of gold and there were flashes of liiiiiight . . ." But, on Celine Dion Sunday, my heart's cry was somehow more passionate and more peaceful at the same time.

". . . and the things of this world will grow strangely dim in the light of His glory and grace . . ."

If you have ever identified yourself with any of the following terms: worry monster, terror hub, anxiety metropolis, fear bishop, or other related terms, you probably don't tend to think of yourself as brave and courageous. But you can wear that identity, because it's your truest one. Your truest identity is that you're God's chosen, rescued, on the way to glorious child. You are a temple of the Holy Spirit and He has all the power. He can give you the courage to love fearlessly, to walk through hard things peacefully, to speak truth into a dark world, or to rest.

You can pursue Him back. You can keep your eyes on Him. You can ask Him to help you. He will. He loves to, because He loves you.

> He did not even spare his own Son but offered him up for us all. How will he not also with him grant us everything? (Rom. 8:32)

THERE SHE IS, TAKE HER!

You know those family stories that make their way around the holiday table over and over again even though they are unbearably embarrassing? The stories where everyone laughs because it was a long time ago. But you were totally the worst, and you're like "Why are we all laughing so much at how terrible I was?"

Well, one of my (non)shining moments happened when I was about twelve and my little sister was only about four. We were at the doctor's office and both due for a shot. Unlike Katniss, the self-sacrificing big sister in *The Hunger Games,* willing to give her own life to protect her little sister from pain and suffering, when the nurse asked, "Okay, who's first?" my arm shot out like a bullet and my stiff finger pointed right at the face of my sweet, chubby-cheeked baby sister. Through tears, I shouted, "TAKE HER!"

Facing down the needle, I sold out my sister. "Take her." I immediately threw my sibling to the immunization sharks, and she took that needle like a brave little soldier. *Sorry, Aubrey.*

So, in my natural, fleshly state, I was not the "Here I am, give me the shots!" type. I was not the "Send me to Africa and bring on the boils!" girl. I was the "take her" sister. I was the "Isn't there someone else who wants to go on the mission trip to the third-world country?" youth group member. The "please accept this nod and silent smile as the extent of my neighborliness while we share a wall in this apartment complex" person.

But, when we look in the Bible, we see ordinary people giving up their lives for Jesus. Look at people like Isaiah, volunteering to go wherever God would have him go.

Isn't that an insane idea? Think about it. If you're an anxious person, it's especially absurd. "God, send me . . . give me a one-way ticket to anywhere you want, even if it's the WORST PLACE on planet Earth!"

How does that happen? What prompts regular Joes to exhibit the kind of courage and soul peace that says "God, I trust WHATEVER you have for me, WHEREVER it is"?

Isaiah 6 is one of my favorite chapters in the Bible. If you look at the subheading at the start of the chapter it says, "Isaiah's Call and Mission."

So, for some context, the chapter starts out stating that King Uzziah died. Apparently, he was one of the hard-to-come-by good ones. But his son was terrible. And so, Uzziah died, and his terrible son was now going to take over. People were probably pretty concerned about the shift in leadership and what it meant for them.

But then we read about Isaiah, who during this transition of earthly kings saw the King of kings—the hem of His robe filling the temple. That's in verse 1.

If you grew up in church, like me, you've probably sung that phrase "and the hem (or train) of his robe filled the temple" in your sleep and done many a Connect-the-Dots Isaiah 6 Sunday school worksheet. But can you actually imagine the reality of what Isaiah saw?

Could you imagine seeing, with your eyeballs, THE God, surrounded by smoke and shouting six-winged angels while standing in an earthquake?

His reaction was appropriate.

"Woe is me for I am ruined . . ." (v. 5).

In some versions, he says the phrase "I am undone!"

In other words, Isaiah's response to seeing the massive glory of Jesus was "AHHHH, I'M DEAD, I'M THE WORST, KILL ME NOW, I AM UNWORTHY."

And then an angel, and I mean, one of these shouting six-wingers flew at him with a hot coal.

(Passes out.)

But the angel didn't attack, he touched his lips with a hot coal and told him that his sin was forgiven.

So crazy.

Isaiah did not do a single thing to deserve that forgiveness.

". . . and your sin is atoned for" (v. 6).

How bizarre.

All we saw him do was cower in terror.

But think about it. All it takes for a person to be saved from their sin is the recognition that "I AM NOT WORTHY," and the mercy of God. Isaiah's response to the presence of the Lord was half humility, half heart attack. Intense, desperate, I-am-nothing humility. And the Lord gave him mercy.

So what does this have to do with fear?

Look at how Isaiah responded to the mercy of God: "Then I heard the voice of the Lord asking: Who should I send? Who will go for us? I said: Here I am. Send me" (Isa. 6:8).

Isaiah didn't do a training camp. He didn't take steroids or attend a seminar on how to be brave. He didn't have to be brave. He simply stood in the presence of God. And being with God, experiencing God, and being *forgiven* by God revolutionized how he saw the world and his place in it. He thought he was going to be unmade. Instead, amazing grace. "Send me anywhere."

That's what Jesus does. If you spend time in His presence, you don't have the brain space to obsess over other lesser things. If you spend time with Jesus, if you see yourself and your world in the shadow of the cross, you find yourself becoming more and more single-minded until the words, "Here I am. Send me" pour out of you like they were in there the whole time.

SINGLE-MINDEDNESS AS A REMEDY

Our minds are divided. I know mine tends toward that. Being focused on ten million stressful things, rather than the one singular thing we can put all our hope in.

I love how Tim Keller put it in a sermon he preached called, "Peace—Overcoming Anxiety." Keller said:

> There's a great place where Martha and Mary, two sisters, have Jesus in to eat, and Martha is running all around, running all around. It says she was *anxious marinus*, with much serving. The word literally means to have her mind divided and distracted and trying to get to too many goals. Mary is just sitting there listening to Jesus.

Keller continues, quoting Jesus and then explaining the scene. He says:

> "Martha, Martha, you are anxious and troubled about many things." Mary has found the one thing needful. Mary is single-minded. Mary has one thing she is looking at. You have 300 things. I'm one of them. That's nice, Martha. I'm glad I'm one of the 300 things you're thinking about, but I'm not offended. You are in trouble until I'm the one thing."

. . . It's because the opposite of anxiety is single-mindedness, and the opposite of peace is worry, and the counterfeit of peace is a kind of apathy and cynicism, and that counterfeit peace cannot coexist with the tenderness of love and joy and so on. How do you cultivate it? Fairly simple. It says, verse 8 [of Philippians 4], "Whatever is true, whatever is noble, whatever is right, think on these things . . ."

What are the 300 things you have your mind on? For me, the list sometimes looks a little like this . . .

- When can I eat chips and green salsa from Blue Coast Burrito again without having a heart attack by the age of thirty-five?
- How is that uncomfortable conversation with that distant relative going to go?
- Do I seem obnoxious on social media? Maybe I should quit everything . . .
- Are my kids doing the right things?
- Am I a bad mom?
- Will I ever work out again?
- What is it that working out entails? I truly can't remember.
- How can I speak life into this very dark situation?

- Am I really speaking life or am I being pious?

Writing that list out was convicting for me. It's incredible how self-centered even a tiny sampling of my 300 things are. Even my "best intentioned" thoughts revolve around the burning questions, *Am I doing things right? Am I a failure? Am I pretty? Are my motives perfect? Am I worthy of being loved?*

God wants us to stop thinking about ourselves so much. He wants us to stop obsessing over the gym and the deadline and the relational tension. He wants our thoughts to be singular. He wants us to think about Him.

He tells us to think about Him in His Word, and He knows that if we are single-minded, if we are spending brain power thinking of Him, preaching the gospel to ourselves, reminding ourselves of the Father's goodness and our already approved status in Christ, only then will we live in freedom from fear. Sorry, boils.

Section 2

MY FEARS WILL NOT DEFEAT ME

Chapter Four

SLEEPING THROUGH ANDREW

• • • • • • • • • • • • • • • • •

I once slept through a Category 5 hurricane.

It was Hurricane Andrew.

The year was 1992 and I was a stressed six-year-old in muggy Miami, swimming and drawing, and letting my tiny maltese, Homer, chase me up and down the tile hallway when I got home from school. My mom had just remarried, and we'd just left Los Angeles. And the home I'd known was gone. The school I'd known was gone. Life felt unpredictable and stormy in every way.

It was a Sunday afternoon when I watched Paul, my new dad, who, remember, had SWAT team muscles, barely break a sweat as he put up hurricane shutters. I saw grownups with scrunched up eyebrows, staring at TV screens, and noticed that everyone seemed to be at the grocery store for water jugs, just like us. I could tell things were strange, but it wasn't clicking to me that this massive, life-threatening storm would, in one day, cause more than $25 billion in damages. I didn't know our city was about to change forever. I didn't understand that this thing was about to travel directly over our little white lakefront townhouse.

At that time, well basically all of the '90s, bedtime was an always-stressful event for me, because I was very concerned about the concept of "a full night's sleep."

I wanted to be at school at 7:30, half an hour early, so I'd have a chance to really settle and be relaxed before class started. Mental preparation was important. If I got thrown into my day all willy-nilly, say 7:55, and had to rush to class, who knows what the day would hold then? WHO KNOWS! Might as well not even wake up for that kind of day.

Waking up this early still required a solid nine hours, because I'd been told by grown-ups that nine hours of sleep a night was important.

So having a morning routine I could count on was a nonnegotiable. But when I learned that what time I fell asleep could have an effect on my trustworthy morning situation, my adrenaline really kicked into high gear. *Go to sleep, Scarlet. Go to sleep, right now, Scarlet. Don't you dare not go to sleep right now, Scarlet. IT'S TEN P.M. ON A SCHOOL NIGHT, SCARLET. SLEEEEEEP!*

So, this obviously became a thing for me. Bedtime stress. I was proficient enough at math to know that if I looked at my digital bedside clock and saw any glowing green numbers that went beyond 9:30 p.m., my solid nine hours would be compromised.

Nights there were extenuating circumstances—a dinner out at a restaurant that went a little late, an episode of *Underdog* sucking me in and making me lose track of time, or simply laying in bed and stressing about the numbers getting closer and closer to 9:30—I'd be in so much turmoil that I'd stay up until almost midnight crying about how I wasn't going to get a solid nine hours. I WASN'T GOING TO GET A SOLID NINE HOURS!

But the eve of Andrew was *not* one of those nights. I crawled into bed at 8:45—plenty of time for comforter-straightening, pillow situating, itching my arms and legs, and wondering what bed bugs looked like and if my bed had them, and praying that the Lord would miraculously remove the bed bugs if I did have them. Back then, other than for bed bug protection, I think my prayers were most frequently that the devil, who for some reason I thought lived in the right-hand corner of my ceiling by the door, wouldn't get me while I slept. But on this night, I dozed off more easily than usual and slept through the most destructive hurricane to ever hit Florida.

When I woke up and went outside, I couldn't see the road we lived on because it was covered in pieces of our neighborhood. My hometown had been crushed while I got my doctor-recommended nine hours.

My sleep was deep and peaceful the night before the storm because I was ignorant. I was unaware of the danger.

Oblivious to the threat. Blind to the reality that storms like Andrew cause death and devastation.

As I wrote this book, Hurricane Harvey, an Andrew-like storm but *bigger,* threatened the people I love in Miami. And I was looking at this big, ominous image that was all over every screen, plowing toward my people, and thinking, *How can we find peace here? There are storms within and storms without. How can any of us feel safe?*

And I remembered we can't. Not on our own, anyway. No chance. We don't get to be safe by ourselves.

We are kids with crumbling dreams. We are palm trees in violent winds. We are weaker than the waters that rise in our lives. We sense we are and we know we are and our fears can feel like a hurricane.

But we are not alone.

Psalm 3:3 (ESV) says, "But you, O LORD, are a shield about me, my glory, and the lifter of my head."

We are not alone because we have a Shield. Our Shield overcame death and every single thing that makes us afraid. He can handle our fears. Our glory is beyond us. It is not the life we've built that can be crushed or washed away. We have a greater glory, sealed forever.

And He is the One who lifts up our heads . . .

When we are afraid, when we are weak, and when we worry about what is to come, we have Someone who gives us His strength. When our children are hurting, when our jobs are taken, when the clock says, "no mercy" at 9:45, we have Someone who pulls us up and meets our gaze. He lifts our chin and while the winds scream of the end of the world, His eyes assure us we are loved.

We can look up and see Jesus.

My Jesus who speaks and makes storms disappear. My Jesus who has already defeated sin and death and everything ominous and scary. My Jesus who loves my friends Little Christy and my Nicole, when they sat in the path of a hurricane in Miami, even more than I love them because they are His.

"And the things of this world will grow strangely dim . . ."

We are not alone. We have a shield, a glory, and a lifter who loves us.

PEACE IN A TORNADO

When I call Brandon, it doesn't say my name on his phone. It says one of my nicknames (Scrawls), followed by a tornado emoji, followed by another one of my nicknames, "Ol' Reliable" (it's an ironic nickname). The picture that flashes up is an off-brand Elmo with fire behind him. Each of those details is attached to different long stories that are probably not interesting, but my point is, tornadoes have always been such a thing for me that I literally have one attached to my name on our phones.

I never lived in any tornado-ish areas until the last five years, but that never stopped me from being terrified of them. They're the worst. They're super creepy looking and deadly and unpredictable. Seriously, you don't know when the death wind is coming for you.

I knew there would be storms on the March day I took my daughters to the donut shop. But I didn't think the bad weather would roll in for several hours. I didn't know tornadoes were a possibility that day. I didn't even think we'd get caught in the rain.

I'd noticed the night before that we were out of coffee, so I decided I would surprise the girls with Dunkin' Donuts (I vastly prefer Krispy Kreme, but parenting is a life of sacrifice) and that I'd treat myself with coffee I didn't have to make.

Because I'd pre-planned this outing, and at the time, I only had two daughters, we were semi-dressed and mostly-clean and out the door in no time.

We pulled in at Dunkin', shuffled inside, and ordered our donuts and coffee. I asked the lady who was helping us how she was doing and she paused before saying, "I'm runnin' . . . but not on Dunkin." I chuckled, because, come on, that's pretty funny. Then I thanked her and took our donuts.

Ever wanted a seat by the huge glass windows, but I said, "Eh, it's supposed to storm soon, so let's sit farther away from the windows."

Almost as soon as we sat down, the sky got weird. Now this particular Dunkin' is ALL windows and it was suddenly ominously dark and it felt like everyone in the store collectively held their breath. I remember saying to Ever,

"Wow. Look at the sky. Maybe we should take these donuts to go . . ."

As soon as I got the words out, the wind threw the door open and our napkins flew everywhere. Then, there was so much hail. My memory says they were the size of tennis balls, but who knows?

It all happened so quickly. The power in the donut shop went off and tornado sirens went on. There were about eight other customers in the store, and all of our iPhones started buzzing at the same time while "TORNADO WARNING: TAKE SHELTER NOW" flashed on our screens. We all instinctively huddled near the bathroom, gawking at the huge, rattling windows, only twenty feet away. It looked like we were inside a black cloud that was rushing by horizontally. The trees were bending into right angles. It was so loud.

A real tornado was really on the other side of the glass, touching down, one street over.

The Dunkin' Donuts lady who was "runnin', but not on Dunkin'" wrapped her arms around my Ever, and we were all silent wondering what would happen next.

I held my girls, and maybe some strangers, and asked God, out loud, to please protect us. Ever was softly crying and shaking and Dewy, only one year old at the time, was motionless, like she knew something was happening but didn't know what to feel. And then, it was like a light switch was flipped. The sky jolted into an instant, eerie stillness. The darkness dissipated. People started moving again.

"Did that just happen?" we all mumbled, "and do these donuts taste better than I remember?"

It wasn't until then that I had time to text Brandon and tell him what was happening. I'd been in a tornado in a Dunkin' Donuts.

So, there it was. One of my biggest fears of my entire life actually happened., The death wind came to the donut shop. And the funny thing is, *I wasn't afraid.* Ever was afraid, and I just kept telling her that God is in control of the weather and He is good and He loves us and we can trust Him. Even when bad things happen, we can trust Him.

It's just so crazy. We don't have to be afraid.

At the time, during that little sliver of life in March 2017, people were constantly asking me if I was nervous about what we were preparing to do that month—fly overseas as a family to adopt little Joy from China. And my answer was no. I wasn't nervous.

The tornado grazed us just weeks before we boarded that plane. And the reason I could sit so calmly as the hail and wind threatened our lives was because I was so confident in the goodness and sovereignty of the God who had been leading me through the exhausting and emotionally-charged ordeal of the adoption process.

I was hyper-aware of the reality that my life can't really end by way of some hail and wind. I'm going to live forever with Jesus in perfect peace.

Those first few months of 2017 are a blur of God coming through. Of God surprising us with provisions and gifts. So, even in the face of an actual tornado, I had peace because the Holy Spirit was ruling my heart. He was interceding for me, giving me that gift of perfect peace, and as I watched a real tornado rattle the doors of the donut shop I was in with my children, I knew that I had a Savior who couldn't be rattled by a little rain.

THE WEIGHT OF THE WIND

> When God fixed the weight of the wind and distributed the water by measure, when he established a limit for the rain and a path for the lighting, he considered wisdom and evaluated it; he established it and examined it. (Job 28:25–27)

Maybe you've heard of Job. He authored the book of Job. He was the one that loved God so much and had an amazing life, until he lost everything. Remember him?

He had the beautiful, bustling family, the land, the animals, and the wealth. And Satan wanted to stick it to God by discrediting Job's love. In Job 1, we read a conversation recorded between God and Satan. When the Lord mentioned Job and how he feared the Lord and walked upright, Satan challenged the idea that Job's love for God was genuine. In verses 10 and 11, Satan suggested that Job didn't really love God, but rather, he loved the stuff from God.

So, God gave Satan permission to take everything away from Job, everything but his own life. God knew Job trusted Him and loved Him and would continue to trust and love Him even after a tornado took the life of his kids.

Satan did the horrible, destructive things he loves to do and ruined Job's life. His wealth, his children, his own health—everything was taken from him. And his wife told him to "Curse God and die" (Job 2:9). So, in just a few chapters in the Bible, we see this man lose every treasure, every comfort, every relationship, every single thing this world has to offer.

Gone. All gone. But, he didn't "curse God and die."

Because *God was right.*

Job wasn't trusting his stuff. Job wasn't even trusting his people. He was trusting his Creator.

Camels were taken. A strong wind caused a house to collapse—the house that contained all his children. Boils came. Job suffered to the brink of physical, emotional, and spiritual death, and yet, he held onto the Lord. He trusted the Creator of the wind, though he didn't understand the way it blew.

John Piper wrote a masterpiece of a poem on the life of Job. It's beautiful and long and made me think about a part of Job's story I never think about—his faith *before* he lost everything.

You've got to read the whole thing for yourself. It's called "The Misery of Job and the Mercy of God"—but just read these few lines, out loud if you can . . .

But Job had seen the years
Change dark and early-morning fears
To pleasant afternoons and clear
Night-skies, star-strewn and bright from
    here
To who knows where beyond the brink
Of earth and heav'n. So Job would drink
His desert-berry wine, and walk
Along his garden paths, and talk
Of all the years that God had made
His fields to bear the golden blade
For camels, oxen, asses, sheep—
Eleven thousand mouths to keep
With grain and grass and streams—and
    not
A flood or drought or wasting rot,
Or pestilence, or early freeze,
Or looting from his enemies
And Job would lift his hands to God,
And wonder why he spared the rod
Of suffering. Each day he blessed
The gentleness of God, confessed
His hope in God alone, and said,
"O Lord, if this were lost instead,
And all I had was you, I would
Be rich, and have the greatest Good. . . ."[7]

I never think about that version of Job. The had-it-made Job. Do you?

I never think about the anxiety he may have sometimes felt, living such a perfect life in such a clearly wounded world—a world where cold-blooded murder between brothers happened in the very first family.

Rather, I used to think Job was living the life, and then he lost everything, and then he didn't curse God and die. And then he died. The end.

But this poem reminded me that Job was a human person who enjoyed all the good things this world can give us—and who knows how often he wondered *why?*

Who knows how many nights he sat up with a neighbor or a friend who was suffering a loss and thought, *Why has the Lord blessed me so? Why does death and disease and pain and agony seem to touch everyone else?*

Job must have appeared, to his peers, to be a lucky son of a gun before it all went down.

I know that for me, anyway, the seasons I'm riding high are often the ones I'm most prone to be anxious. The seasons when the wind is kissing my face just right, and the temperature outside and inside is that perfect mid-60s, low-70s crisp, and the storms are an ocean away—that's when I'm afraid. That's when I tend to take my eyes off the Lord and focus in on the wind. I wonder when it's coming. How hard will it hit?

When you're squinting in the storm and the rain is so heavy you can't see what's in front of you, it's not scary so much as it is difficult.

A RAIN STORM AT VBS

When Joy had only been home a few weeks, I put my oldest into a Vacation Bible School camp. She loved it and learned songs about Jesus and got a T-shirt with a rocket ship on it, and I was still learning how to get two toddlers into and out of a church building at the correct times every day.

On day three or four there was a huge rainstorm. I pulled up to the church building with my two- and four-year-olds, both the same size at the time because Joy was still recovering from her early malnourishment, and I looked at the door I was supposed to walk through that looked a thousand miles and a million gallons away and I mumbled, "How . . ."

I didn't have a double stroller and I'd forgotten all the contraptions at home. So, I knew I just had to get the girls out, put one in the umbrella stroller, and jog through the rainstorm clutching the other one to try to get my oldest in time.

As soon as I got out of the car, I was instantly drenched and I knew I was doomed. I pulled the umbrella stroller out of the trunk and—I'm not even kidding you right now—the stroller was ripped out of my hands by a gust of wind and thrown to the other side of the parking lot. I thought, *So this is how it ends*, and fought the deep urge to fetal up in the parking lot. What felt like years later, I stumbled into the building with one toddler under each arm. Both soaking wet. All of us crying.

The wind and the rain overwhelmed us all. And I could barely see beyond that moment.

That happens to me so often. The hard storm in front of me is what gets my attention, rather than the God who weighs the wind above it all.

It doesn't seem possible for the frazzled, dripping wet mom to enter the sea of VBS strangers with grace. Wetness and crying don't seem to lead to graciousness when you're the wet, crying one. But we made it. And we laughed about it. I'm pretty sure I didn't say any swear words. I'm pretty sure I left the building with all my children and at least a sliver of my sanity.

And that's the whole thing, you guys. We can walk through flooded parking lots with screaming children hanging off of our every limb without falling apart. We can pass through the huge Job storms and the small VBS storms because we are in the care of the Master of the storms. We have grace even when we don't feel gracious.

If our gaze pierces through the ceiling and the storm clouds and lingers on the love of a God who is calm and controlled and beaming at us with love, no wetness or wind or stroller hurled about can truly rattle us.

"THINGS ARE TOO GOOD" FEAR

I used to only identify with Job during seasons of sharp suffering, but when it comes to fear, the seasons in which I battle the most are the seasons that feel too good to be true. Maybe the same was true of Job.

When things in my life are just click-click-clicking along, I look out across the street, across the aisle, across the Instagram feed and see pained people with hashtags that are less #blessed and more #struggle and I think to myself, *I must be next* . . . I should feel for them, but instead I feel for me. What a selfish heart I have . . .

I think it's easy though, to see suffering and think about how it affects you. And I wonder if Job did live with a small sense of foreboding. That's what it's like here in this often sad, sometimes scary place, after all. We hope for heaven and we endure suffering; and when we're not enduring it, we're seeing it all around us and waiting for the tornado to interrupt our donut date.

But, oh my goodness, there is so much beauty here. There is beauty in our position. We get the luxury of knowing how this thing ends. We get the peaceful privilege of looking back at a cross that tells us who we are, so that when we look ahead, we know where we'll be. We get the gift of knowing that it's not up to us or up to a lucky hand to make things right. We can actually rest, relieved, knowing that nothing we've done makes God love us any less and nothing we can do will make God love us any more. We don't decide our safeness. And we've already seen the full measure of love from the One who does.

My pastor, Josh Howerton, puts it this way, "The gospel is this message that you are so bad that Jesus had to die for you, but you are so loved by God that He was glad to die for you. God does not simply love some future, better version of you. He loves you now, in all of your jacked-up-ness."

I love that God loves to handle "jacked-up-ness."

Embracing that message while you're in pain AND while you're sitting in peace and looking out at pain, is what it's all about. That is why Job could be crushed without cursing God.

SUICIDAL JOB

Job was a human being, and he responded to his catastrophes with humble, human anguish. In chapter 10, he told his friend, Bildad, some of the things he'd told God, one of them being, "Why did you bring me out of the womb? I should have died and never been seen. I wish I had never existed but had been carried from the womb to the grave" (vv. 18–19).

Psychiatrists these days would call that "passively suicidal." He didn't have a suicide plan written up, but he didn't want to exist anymore either. He felt the sorrow of his losses and it buried his desire to live. And he was honest about it. He wasn't what we'd look at today as the "Super Christian" who suffers and shows up Sunday morning with a plastered smile on their face.

He felt real, raw, terrible things. He said those things. He may have screamed those things. And yet he did not cease trusting God.

Go back a few pages to the beginning of this chapter and re-read what Job says about God in chapter 28.

"When God *fixed the weight* of the
wind . . ."

"When he *established a limit for the rain* . . ."

Do you see that? Do you see the wisdom in Job's
words? Job is recognizing, even in his grief, even when he
can't wrap his mind around the *why* of what his life has
become, that God is the One who "fixed the weight of the
wind" and "established a limit for the rain."

What is Job saying here? He's saying that God is in
control. He's saying that he knows God made all things
and rules over all things.

If you take the time to read through the book of Job,
you'll notice that his words often sound a lot like words
from people who don't have a book of the Bible named
after them. They sound like familiar responses to pain. He
was devastated. He was depressed. He was confused.

Have you ever looked at your life and said, "God . . .
why! Why did You allow this to happen?"

Job did too, but in all his words, in his tears, in his
prayers, in his conversations with friends, he acknowledged
that though he couldn't understand why his greatest fears
had been made real, he never once denied God's all-know-
ing, all-powerful, all-good nature.

WEATHERING LIFE

When I think of weather (tornadoes) and fear of
weather (tornadoes and firenadoes), I don't think of just

storms, but of all the little life moments we can't control. The ones that strike us suddenly and cripplingly. The ones we couldn't have prevented. The moments that knock the wind out of us when we weren't prepared for the punch. The lay-offs. The breakups. The diagnosis. The sudden deaths.

We can't good-works our way out, or gluten-free our way around, or even pray a path to avoid the unexpected bad. But we can trust that even when we are surprised by the lightning bolt of pain, by the hurricane of sadness, by the blizzard of relational strain when we forgot our jacket and our thicker skin, God is not surprised. He fixed the weight of the wind.

He knows this world inside and out because He made it out of nothing.

He knows you, and the number of hairs on your head, and the things you're terrified of losing or gaining. He knows everything you've ever done and everything you'll ever do. He watched it all happen, experiencing your storms on the cross and He chose to hold your future in His hands. And so, if you're His beloved child, your future is glory.

> For I consider that the sufferings of this
> present time are not worth comparing with
> the glory that is going to be revealed to us.
> (Rom. 8:18)

It's just an incredible thing, the Christian life. I look back at the layers and layers of sin and fear and disobedience that Jesus has pulled me out of and I am in awe. He has proven over and over again that He is enough. He has showed me in sickness and in sadness and even in the middle of a tornado in Dunkin' Donuts, that my fears cannot defeat me. He has already died for their demise and for the glory that will be revealed in me. So instead, I'm in awe, as I experience this gift He loves to give His children—the gift of perfect peace.

> You will keep the mind that is dependent on You in perfect peace, for it is trusting in You. (Isa. 26:3)

GOD OFTEN GIVES "MORE THAN YOU CAN HANDLE"

The longer you live, the more you will see that we often find ourselves walking through circumstances that are more than we can handle. The so-called verse that became a Christian cliche, "God will never give you more than you can handle," is not actually a verse and isn't actually true. We all know it. We often have to walk through way more than we can handle. And in those moments, we have the opportunity to take our fears, our pain, our broken hearts to a God who *absolutely can* handle it.

First Corinthians 10:13 says, "But God is faithful; he will not allow you to be tempted beyond what you are able, but with the temptation he will also provide a way out so that you may be able to bear it." There is only a way to bear it because there is a way out, and there is only a way out because there is a Faithful One who makes a way. We can really bear very little, "but God is . . ."

Like Job, there is the chance that this broken world, wrecked by sin, desperate to be made right again, could take everything we love from us. It can even take you. What if everyone you love is in that one car that wrecks on the interstate? What if the wildfire is so widespread, there's nowhere to go and no rescuer in sight? What if bad guys finally do ignore the ADT sign and break in? Your body may go into fight or flight, and your heart may palpitate, but your soul can rest. It can. It can rest because it can't be destroyed. If the car wrecks or the fire wins or the bad guys are faster than you, your earthly, dead body will raise to new life in resurrected glory, in the perfect state that nothing can touch, in a better, forever, everlasting home. And you'll stand in front of the Book of Life and your eye will catch, and you'll say, "That's my name."

If you haven't experienced the adrenaline-through-the-roof feeling, the heart-so-heavy-it-might-fall-out-of-your-body feeling, or the I'm-so-confused-that-I wish-I'd-never-existed feeling, you will.

Because we still live here in the broken place. And we still have an enemy that wants us to be tunnel-visioned on the brokenness so that we'll be scared and we'll stop trusting God.

We have hurricanes and tornadoes and broken hearts and hard days. But they all retreat to the shadows in the light of the cross. It's hard to be afraid when you're looking

past the forecast. It's hard to be focused on what's temporary when Jesus lifts your head.

Jesus, the Prince of Peace, is more powerful than any
storm we'll face and we are His.

We don't have to think about, study, in-the-shower-talk,
or email-draft our fears. They cannot withstand Christ so
they cannot defeat us. Jesus has already defeated everything we fear on the cross.

PRAYER OR PILLS?

There have been a few times when I've been so physically affected by my anxiety that I went on medication.
During those seasons, I'd find myself seeking the Lord,
hearing from Him through His Word, feeling emotionally fine in a lot of ways, and yet hyperventilating my way
through each day. I felt physically wound-up even if I felt
spiritually focused.

And the medication helped. I want you to know this
because I want you to know that I'm not a "prayer AND
PRAYER ALONE is the answer for anxiety" type of
person.

Tim Keller preached a sermon back in 2004 called,
"The Wounded Spirit." He posed some questions such as,
"What goes wrong with a spirit? . . . Why do our emotions
and our feelings seem to get out of control? . . . Why do we
struggle so much? What is our problem?"

Then, he said, ". . . you know what the biblical answer
is? It's complicated."

Keller suggests that the Bible's answer to these questions is more complex and nuanced than any other counseling model or book. Self-help books say it's all emotional. Psychiatric nurse practitioners who prescribe medicine say it's all physical. Christians, generalized, say it's all moral (Are you reading your Bible? Are you in sin? How is your "quiet time"?).

Keller poses the idea that most people think there is one simple solution to anxiety. And that these solutions are "one dimensional" and "reductionistic" and "simple minded."

You've got to hear this sermon. Really. He uses Scripture to look at all the factors that can contribute to what he calls, "A wounded spirit." And using the book of Proverbs, he lays out all the different contributing factors to the wounded spirit.

There's the physical aspect. Your anxiety can absolutely be attributed to brain chemical imbalance or not eating right or even a thyroid issue.

There's the emotional/relational aspect. Maybe you're anxious because you need the love of a friend. In this case, medicine won't help you.

There's a moral aspect. Your conscience. If you're living in sin, the Bible says you'll "flee though no one pursues" (Prov. 28:1 NIV). So, eating healthy won't help this issue.

There's an existential aspect. Everyone knows that the party ends—people you love will die—death takes everything you treasure in this world. "Even in laughter, a heart may be sad, and joy may end in grief" (Prov. 14:13).

And of course, there's the faith aspect. A faith-related anxiety cannot be cured with medicine or thyroid hormone or coming to terms with your fear of death. Keller finished the sermon by showing how the cross speaks to every root of a wounded spirit. It is beautiful.

But we need to understand there is no simple one-way to look at anxiety. You and I are different. Some of us were raised by cops. Some of us have faulty thyroids. Some of us are doubting that the Lord is good. Some of us are all of it wrapped up together.

Being on brain medicine was a humbling experience for me. I cycled through feelings of shame. I obsessed over my tired thought that if I were "a better Christian," I wouldn't need medicine. But the Lord showed me so much grace in those seasons. He reminded me through His Word and through the grace of friends that He is for me. He loves me. He made it clear that I can't earn or lose His love based on whether or not I take a pill, whether or not I read my Bible every day at 5:11 a.m., whether or not I exhibit peace and joy a greater percentage of my day.

I had a Christian counselor in my early twenties who prescribed me some anxiety pills and tried to talk me down from the shame I felt over it by comparing me to a diabetic.

She said something like "Would you feel embarrassed if you had to take insulin because your pancreas wasn't working as it should? The brain is an organ just like the pancreas, and who is going to criticize a diabetic for taking the insulin they need to manage their blood sugar and not die? Mental health management has a stigma, but it shouldn't. If there is a pill that can help you stop hyperventilating all day, you should take it."

Those little white pills helped me with the physical aspect of my anxiety, but they weren't a cure-all. They only helped my struggle in one way and made it easier to remember the more important provision that has been made for me in Jesus.

Now, on the other side of it all, I can tell you that I won't be surprised if I find myself dealing with emotional or physical or even moral anxiety again, but I've learned that the gospel can stand up to any fears.

JESUS' PRESCRIPTION

No matter where you suspect your anxiety might stem from, you should always be looking to God's Word, because as you seek Jesus, He brings you the assurance of your faith, which is more potent than any other prescription.

Do you know what Jesus prescribes for the anxious heart?

Prayer.

> Don't worry about anything, but in everything, through prayer and petition with thanksgiving, present your requests to God. And the peace of God, which surpasses all understanding, will guard your hearts and minds in Christ Jesus. (Phil. 4:6–7)

If you view "prayer and petition" as a dumping of wishes on a God capable of literally anything, you'll likely feel that common frustration of having your "prayers bounce off the ceiling."

God didn't create you to get your grocery list. He wants your heart. He wants to communicate with you. He is absolutely ready for your "rawness." I mean, He knows what you're feeling already.

Read through the Psalms and see all the emotions David prayed through. Especially the one I keep mentioning where he calls God the "lifter of his head" in Psalm 3:3 (ESV).

> LORD, how my foes increase! There are many who attack me. . . . I cry aloud to the LORD, and he answers me from his holy mountain. . . . Rise up, LORD! Save me, my God! You strike all my enemies on the cheek; you break the teeth of the wicked. . . . (vv. 1, 4, 7)

Crying aloud in desperation, talking about his enemies and "broken teeth." That's intense. If you were sitting on an unfamiliar couch in someone's living room for a Bible study and they prayed that way, you might sneak out the door before they said "amen."

If you ever feel like you're "too emotional," just read the Psalms. Read what David, the guy (sinner, murderer, adulterer, king) that God called "a man after his own heart" has to say. He says crazy emo things!

I've never prayed that the people I didn't like would have broken teeth. Have you?

David talked to God about his sadness and his fear and his joys and even his anger. He didn't say, "Thanks for this food. Can I have a raise?" He quoted Scripture in his prayers and told God how he was feeling in his prayers and he didn't hide his doubts and depression from God. He truly cast his cares on God.

Our prayers feel like they're going nowhere when we forget Who we're talking to. When we're praying to feel something or to get something or forget something, we're not going to experience the peace that comes from inter-acting with our made-everything, sustains-everything, still-has-time-to-listen Creator.

When we remember that we have a God that loves to the death, a God that was wounded so He could heal, a God that listens and sacrifices and responds, we can't help but be honest and trust His good heart.

I was on a Francis Chan YouTube binge recently, and before he started a sermon, he paused to talk about a con-versation he'd had recently. Someone asked him what his favorite part of being a Christian was, and he said respond-ing was easy. The best thing about being a Christian is answered prayer.

He went on, gushing about what a wonder it is to know that you can say things to God—Creator of everything—and that He hears and things change. There's just nothing more comforting, nothing more powerful, nothing more reassuring than that.

If we're not praying relationally, in an attempt to know and love our God, if rather we're praying in an attempt to fix ourselves, while we're running toward our fears, we waste our breath.

God is full of mercy, but He wants your heart. He wants your repentance. He doesn't want you to come to Him with bloody hands and feet that race to do wrong (Prov. 6:17–18) and talk to Him like He's a genie in a lamp. The Lord hears the prayers of the humble, the weak, the ones who need Him (all of us) and who know it.

> Humble yourselves before the Lord, and he
> will exalt you. (James 4:10)

When you're afraid, when you're overcome with anxiety, when your faith feels weak, when your body feels shaky, remember Who you're talking to. Remember that God changes things and changes you and never changes.

TORNADOES CAN TAKE LIVES, BUT FEAR HAS BEEN DEFEATED

A tornado could take your home some day. It could. Depending on where you live, a hurricane could crush your property and injure your family. It's possible. Sinkholes open up, wildfires rage, and earthquakes split the ground.

But guess what? Your fears cannot defeat you. Everything you're afraid of has been defeated already. The planet that can be so scary already knows it is broken and the Bible says in Romans 8 that it is crying out to be redeemed. Even the sinkhole knows Jesus is the answer.

When you're having trouble praying, having trouble feeling the awe and wonder of the Jesus who answers your prayers, flip to Mark 4 and read about when Jesus calmed a storm.

The waves rose and crashed on the boat. The clouds boiled and banged, and lightning probably lit up the sky in bolts, each one communicating something like, "You are powerless . . . death is coming . . . and you're a goner" to the hearts of the disciples.

And what was Jesus doing? Napping.

He wasn't sleeping through the storm because of ignorance, the way I slept through a Category 5 hurricane as a six-year-old. He wasn't sleeping because He didn't know what was going on and didn't know to be afraid. He was sleeping because He saw beyond what was going on. He knew how the storm started and how it would stop. He was sleeping because He was confident and He was in control.

His friends didn't get it. Look at how they woke Him up: "Teacher! Don't you care that we're going to die?" (Mark 4:38).

He didn't even respond to His friends. Instead, He got up and talked to the deadly storm like it was an unruly toddler in the middle of a fit at Target.

He said, "Silence! Be still!" (v. 39).

And the Bible tells us that the wind stopped and there was "a great calm." Imminent death. Three words. Great calm.

> The men were amazed and asked, "What
> kind of man is this? Even the winds and the
> sea obey him!" (Matt. 8:27)

We are so quick to act like the disciples. To forget that
the God we're wanting to help us, the God we're wanting
to take care of us, the God we're begging for answers, is the
Commander of storms. He is always at peace because He
is always in charge.

And that peace is ours. It has been given to us. The
same Jesus who spoke a storm to nothing said this to His
disciples before He left.

> "Peace I leave with you. My peace I give to
> you. I do not give to you as the world gives.
> Don't let your heart be troubled or fearful."
> (John 14:27)

So we can be peaceful too, because we know that God
loves us. And we can ask Him for help and He can do what
we can't and say, "Silence" to the storms in our lives.

Unlike my blonde toddler who seems to think most
of my commands are suggestions, the wind and the waves
must obey the commands of the Most High.

> "Even the wind and the sea obey him!"
> (Mark 4:41)

You can trust Jesus with your marriage. You can trust
Him with your diagnosis. You can trust Him with your
children. Your finances. Your career. Your home.

Hurricane hunkering and tornado warnings are sobering things, but you can feel joy and peace in your soul, in the midst of any storm, both literal and figurative.

You know why?

> When he thunders, the waters in the heavens are in turmoil, and he causes the clouds to rise from the ends of the earth. He makes lightning for the rain and brings the wind from his storehouses. (Jer. 10:13)

You can sleep through storms, not in ignorance, but in peace, because the One who controls the weather and the world loves you to the cross and back.

He wins. He already has. Forever He will. He is the author of everything good. He makes everything new. And He is our hope.

If you're bracing for a storm, or if you're absolutely drowning in your fear of one, just look up. The lifter of your head, the lover of your heart, and the shield of your soul faced the greatest storm the world has ever known so that you can rest. He did it and it is already finished. For you.

> I will both lie down and sleep in peace, for you alone, LORD, make me live in safety. (Ps. 4:8)

Chapter Five

"CANCER—CANCER? LIKE, BALD . . . CHEMO CANCER?"

• • • • • • • • • • • • • • • • • •

When I was in high school, my dad gave my mom the nickname "Alpha Dog." An alpha dog is the dominant dog in a pack setting. Mom has always been just that. The strong one in the family—which is funny considering Paul's background in SWAT. My dad is still ripped. And had his pinky shot off. Have I already told you that multiple times? Well, it's an important detail, okay? He's tough. But, when we think strong, we think Mom.

Oh, you need to get a Baby Grand up a narrow staircase? The movers can't figure it out? She'll do it herself. She'll head-butt a hole in the ceiling to get it in if she has to.

When she was a teenager and her dad asked her what career path she wanted to take, she said "I want to be Maria in *The Sound of Music*." So, she moved to Hollywood and she actually made it (not as Maria von Trapp, but as an actress). She goes and she gets. She takes many things by many storms. But a few years ago, she got diagnosed with stage three breast cancer.

Until then, cancer had never really touched our family. I'd had a legitimate cancer *scare* at that point, and of course, many illegitimate cancer scares. But, the real thing was different than the scares. The hardest part of it all, being the loved one of a family member with cancer, is most definitely the fear.

Somehow, after months of learning cancer and talking cancer and fearing cancer, bright red poison dripping into tubes that drip into your mom on your thirtieth birthday starts to feel normal. But what never feels normal is the dark cloud hovering overhead of everything in life. What I never got used to, during her year of treatment, was the never-ending string of questions I'd ruminate on.

Is my mom going to die? Is she okay right now? Am I supposed to ask her if she's okay? What if she's not okay? What does "not okay" even look like? Does she want me to help her change her bandages? Would she tell me she wanted me to help her if she did? Should I ask?

It was strange and scary and felt like a glitch in reality, watching the alpha dog get weaker and go bald and be different. She didn't want us around on the days she was violently sick. I went to see her after her second or third chemo treatment and she was so weak she couldn't lift the remote and didn't remember how to open Facebook on her computer.

After a few more times, I was her ride home from chemo. I had never been to the chemo place before because they don't allow kids and my little entourage was 100 percent comprised of kids. But, being in that place, seeing the tubes and the other bald women and the bright red poison (which some of the nurses call "the red devil") kind of knocked the wind out of me.

I passed hairless people with tired faces. Hairless people with stoic faces. Hairless people with hopeless faces. The hallway into the "Infusion Clinic" might as well have been labeled "Valley of the Shadow of Death."

And then there was my mom. In her curly rainbow wig with her red-rimmed glasses, her Bible on her lap, and a big smile, showing the world how to walk through it.

I kept thinking about Psalm 23, which until the cancerthing sometimes felt like a tired and worn-out psalm I learned as a little kid. Sure, sure, peace, green fields, still waters.

The words took on new meaning for me, though, after watching my mom walk through something so dark with grace and sprightliness.

> The LORD is my shepherd; I shall not want.
> He makes me lie down in green pastures.
> He leads me beside still waters. He restores
> my soul. He leads me in paths of righteous-
> ness for his name's sake. Even though I walk
> through the valley of the shadow of death,
> *I will fear no evil*, for you are with me; your

rod and your staff, they comfort me. You
prepare a table before me in the presence
of my enemies; you anoint my head with
oil; my cup overflows. Surely goodness and
mercy shall follow me all the days of my life,
and I shall dwell in the house of the LORD
forever. (Ps. 23 ESV, emphasis added)

Cancer wasn't easy for my mom and she didn't carry
as much heavy furniture around as she had before. But
something I learned from being on the sidelines, from wit-
nessing her before, during, and after cancer, was that her
strength wasn't hers. It wasn't something she conjured up.
Her strength came from somewhere else. Someone else.

In a commentary by Charles Spurgeon on this familiar
psalm, he started out, "I hope we all know this Psalm by
heart, may we also know it by heart-experience."[8]

When I think of Psalm 23, and my own heart-experience with it, I think of my two big brushes with cancer. I
think about watching the Lord lead my mother beside still
waters while she sat on a mauve chair designed for poison
drips. And I think about my own cancer scare. The legitimate one.

MY "CANCER BABY"

Nashville was gray and drippy. I stood on the rooftop of
the parking garage at Vanderbilt, fixated on the memory of
the sympathetic, furrowed brows of the oncologists who'd

just smeared petroleum jelly and ultrasound equipment all over me while whispering about my tumor before sending me on my way. They'd talked to me and about me so delicately. And then, bye! They released me with no verdict.

Like, I was supposed to just walk to my car like normal after that.

So, I did. Because that's what you do. You walk to your car after that.

I only had one daughter at the time, and she was at home with my parents. And I lingered on the rainy rooftop of the hospital. I stood up there alone and felt the rain hit my face and thought, *Why not me? Doctors at this place deliver news like this every day.*

I could see men in orange neon vests jackhammering concrete, just living their lives like nothing morbid and potentially life-altering had just happened.

It's weird to actually receive ominous health news when you've been bracing yourself for ominous health news your entire life. People who don't battle anxiety usually describe receiving a scary diagnosis like it's a gut punch. Out of the blue. A sudden sinking feeling.

What's weird about having anxiety over something and then walking through that very thing, is that it *still* feels like a gut punch. It *still* feels out of the blue.

Sure, I may have grown up binge-reading encyclopedias on infectious diseases and having false-alarm appendix ruptures and memorizing the WebMD Symptom checker as soon as it became a thing, but I don't think you can really be prepared for the word *cancer*.

When my doctor said the words "oncologist" and "rapidly growing tumors" and "cancer," I responded, totally like a grown-up, "You mean cancer-cancer? Like, bald . . . chemo cancer?"

She said, "Yes. If the results of the biopsy test positive, you'll start chemo on Monday."

It was very odd. I was actually at my OB/GYN's office, because I was pregnant. I'd had a life-threatening failed pregnancy in the past, so I was a closely monitored pregnant person. And things were pretty weird, right out of the gate. My hormone levels were too high, too soon. So, the doctor's hopeful guess was twins! The more ominous guess was a second ectopic pregnancy.

The diagnosis went back and forth from day to day, ultrasound to ultrasound, until the doctors saw something growing in my uterus that was not a baby. Growing very rapidly. Like, every day it was drastically larger.

Then, I learned the terms "molar pregnancy" and "choriocarcinoma."

The doctors thought that what began as a molar pregnancy may have turned into a rare form of rapidly spreading cancer that forms during pregnancy. It was all very bizarre. So, they surgically removed the fast-growing non-baby that was growing in the baby-growing zone and biopsied it.

It was interesting timing, this scare. As God would have it, this life moment happened to fall on the same weekend I'd invited an unbelieving family member, who doesn't know the Lord, to come visit. It was a surreal two-day window that I was awaiting the phone call—the biopsy results—the call that would determine whether I could keep being an energetic young mom or whether I was about to morph into a *weak* cancer patient in an infusion ward.

I said to Brandon, "Surely, God will understand if I cancel the visit . . . with everything that's going on . . ."

And as soon as the words came out of my mouth, I felt this deep and supernatural peace from the Holy Spirit paired with an urgency to be used by Him, and I finished my sentence saying, "No . . . he needs to come. Maybe God timed it this way on purpose . . ."

So, my unbelieving family member showed up. And it was almost like I was floating overhead watching my own self be this creature I didn't recognize. In the midst of recovering from my minor surgical procedure and the terrifying wait for biopsy news, I was like a kite floating over the whole situation—happy and breezy and peaceful. I invited him into my home and he played with my three-year-old. And we ate chips and queso at the best Mexican place in town. And then we found ourselves back in my townhouse, reclining on the couch and he looked at me, shook his head, and said, "How are you so calm right now? You are so awesome."

And miracle of miracles, I was able to respond, through laughter, "No no! YOU KNOW ME! I'm not this. I'm not naturally calm. I can't conjure up this peace. This is the power of Jesus."

And I sat in my living room with this lost man I was tied to by blood, who had brought me so much pain throughout my life, and the Holy Spirit quite literally taught me at that very hour what should be said (Luke 12:12).

Bible verses I didn't even know I knew spilled out of me.

> When I am afraid, I will trust in you. (Ps. 56:3)

> I sought the LORD, and he answered me
> and rescued me from all my fears. (Ps. 34:4)

I talked about Jesus—who He was in my life and why He mattered for my unbelieving family member's life. I told him about when Jesus was on Earth doing His ministry, healing people all over the place, and even raising a twelve-year-old dead girl back to life.

> While he was still speaking, people came from the synagogue leader's house and said, "Your daughter is dead. Why bother the teacher anymore?" When Jesus overheard what was said, he told the synagogue leader, "Don't be afraid. Only believe." . . .
>
> Then he took the child by the hand and said to her, "Talitha koum" (which is translated "Little girl, I say to you, get up"). Immediately the girl got up and began to walk. (She was twelve years old.) At this they were utterly astounded. (Mark 5:35–36, 41–42)

I told him about other people Jesus healed, like Peter's mother-in-law in Matthew 8.

> Jesus went into Peter's house and saw his mother-in-law lying in bed with a fever. So he touched her hand, and the fever left her. Then she got up and began to serve him. (Matt. 8:14–15)

I explained how people in the Bible, like Peter's mother-in-law, responded to the healing of the Lord with a desire to serve Him and told him that Jesus came to heal the world of its sin and He had healed me from hopelessness and that's why I had peace. He'd brought me, like the little girl, from spiritual death to life. *Talitha koum*, Scarlet.

I told him of all the sin and sickness the Lord had healed me from, freed me from, and how He came into this broken world so that we could be forgiven and have peace with God.

I explained to my unbelieving family member that the reason I was peaceful as I waited for a phone call that could contain the words "You have cancer" in it, was because I knew the God who could touch a hand and heal. I knew the God with power over not just sickness and disease, but death itself.

I had tried to share my faith with him in the past. And he usually responded negatively. He didn't want to listen, before. But, free tidbit—people are more apt to listen when you probably have cancer. Especially if you're behaving with emotions that don't match the situation—behaving in unnatural ways, supernatural ways.

I wrote this little update to my friends after the cancer scare about the whole ordeal and the supernatural peace that the Holy Spirit gifted me with that weekend:

> August 27, 2013
>
> Every day has its own reasons to give God glory, but today is one I've got to share . . . I've spent the last two weeks being pricked and scanned almost every day—like a patient on "House"—a mystery. Friday night, I had surgery to remove what I was told was a possibly cancerous tumor. Every day has been an up or down on a roller coaster . . . two weeks ago, doctors thought I was having my second ectopic pregnancy (but an abdominal one). Then, they thought healthy twins. Then, they thought molar pregnancy. Then, they thought cancerous tumor caused by molar pregnancy. Then back to twins. Then, just two days ago, we were talking about starting chemo this week because my blood tests showed numbers that just didn't make sense with any scenarios.
>
> The incredible thing is that God took ME—the most anxiety-prone, nervously-wired person you've probably ever met (y'all

know me)—and gave me the most inexplicable PEACE I've never experienced.

"And the peace of God, which transcends all understanding, will guard your hearts and your minds in Christ Jesus" (Phil. 4:7 NIV).

I never questioned Him. I wasn't angry. I didn't wonder why. I was sad, but I had a strength that I knew wasn't my own.

I know that what I went through in 2010 with the ectopic pregnancy built my faith and taught me how to trust God. And I also know that He gave me strength these past few weeks because a lot of you have been praying for me. Also amazing is the fact that this cancer-scare happened to fall on the three-day window that I was with an unsaved family member. Today, after we got the call that it wasn't cancer, he commented on my "maturity" and how "well I handled the situation" and I got to tell him that I am NOT mature or CALM or STRONG and that what he saw in me was because of Jesus Christ and the strength He's given me.

Grateful to have had that opportunity and to have gotten good news today. No cancer. No molar. Just a strange miscarriage that looked like a tumor. The best-case scenario for a bad scenario. I can move on with my life now and I am just freshly in awe of my great God who strengthens and comforts . . . and provides and heals. Mourning the loss of a second sweet baby today, but so grateful that right now, I get to continue being a healthy Mommy to Ever Grace and wife to Brandon.

God is merciful and gracious and GOOD and even if I had gotten bad news today, He still would be all those things.

That family member of mine still doesn't know Jesus, from what I know. But on the heels of that trip, he was open to listening. He allowed me to share what Jesus had done in my life and for the world, and he listened and he asked questions and he even read a few Bible verses.

God allowed me to walk through something I'd always been scared of, but He gave me the gift of peace in the midst of it. And He used that peace and made it into a tool I was able to use to share His good news with someone I love who needs it.

THE GIFT OF "WEAK"

Being strong feels so good. Before I had kids, I used to run three miles a day and I was a spin instructor. HAHAHAHAHAH. Sorry, I'm just laughing because *who was that person?* Hopefully, by the time you read this, I will have returned to my healthy habits of years past.

But, anyway, once upon a time I ran and spun and went to the gym for more than just the free babysitting. And I felt strong.

But there were other times when I felt weak. For example, when I had to have open abdominal exploratory surgery (more on that in chapter 6), and I couldn't walk or bathe myself or bend over or even sit up in bed—that was a weak point. It didn't feel awesome.

I'm sure you can relate. And I'm sure you can think of other times you felt emotionally powerful or mentally frail.

When I think about fear, what it feels like, what it does to me, one word comes to mind—WEAK. Weak-minded. Weak-willed. Weak. Weak. Weak.

So, where is the beauty in that? Why did Paul (not my dad, but Saul-turned-Paul, the Bible one) "take pleasure in weakness"?

In 2 Corinthians 12, Paul talked about his "thorn in the flesh." No one knows specifically what he was referring to there, but it was obviously a bummer. It was something he struggled with, suffered through, and wished would go away. We all have those things. Paul writes that he begged God three times to take his thorn away, but God didn't do it. Read below, the words God spoke to Paul:

> But he said to me, "My grace is sufficient for you, for my power is perfected in weakness." Therefore, I will most gladly boast all the more about my weaknesses, so that Christ's power may reside in me. So I take

pleasure in weaknesses, insults, hardships, persecutions, and in difficulties, for the sake of Christ. For when I am weak, then I am strong. (2 Cor. 12:9–10)

Do you know what I love about this? Paul isn't the brilliant mastermind who figured out that his thorn remained to keep him humble. The Lord actually told him. During prayer. Paul asked God to take away the weakness, the thorn, the ailment, the flaw, the whatever it was, and God told him no and gave him a reason. "My power is perfected in weakness."

God knows us. He knows how much we like to be liked and admired and applauded, and how we are more concerned with that than people finding healing through the power of the cross. He knows we are greedy, self-centered little creatures wooed by pride who don't want to admit how much we enjoy the feeling of being "puffed up." He knows how deeply we can drink the spinning instruction power.

Everyone likes feeling validated—whether it's a social media response or a promotion or a rave review or a pat on the back or a "thank you, Mommy." We want to feel like all of our running around on our hamster wheels is noticed and appreciated and valuable.

But the Lord knows that ultimately this is a never-satisfying, soul-crushing pursuit. The Lord knows that we are only satisfied and peaceful when we are exalting Him, rather than exalting ourselves.

In an article entitled, "Paul: I Am Content with Weakness," author Jon Bloom writes, "Our fallen nature craves self-glory. We seek the admiration of others. We love the myth of the superhero because we want to be one. So we want our successes to be known and our failures hidden. And since people who achieve remarkable things earn the favor of others, we are tempted to believe that they earn the favor of God as well. That's the last thing Paul wants us to believe. Paul knew better than most that it is not human achievements that showcase the grace of God. It is human helplessness."[9]

Human helplessness.

Weakness.

Being weak, by itself, is a drag. However, fainting from weakness into the strong arms of a loving God is maybe the most wonderful feeling on Earth. We are pushed and bruised and strained, because we live on a planet with gravity and brokenness and pokey things. But, because of the cross, where Jesus was already weak like we deserved to be and strong like we could never be, our spirits can rest all day every day in His strength.

Embracing our weakness and living in full dependence of God's strength is life-changing. I'm learning that being weak and held feels even better than the illusion of "strong."

Oftentimes, it's in our weakest moments that we most tangibly feel the nearness of God. Oftentimes, it's in our weakest moments that we are able to display the strength and the power of God in a way that directs glory upward and away from ourselves.

If you can take the weakness that you feel in the midst of your fear, in the midst of your fretting, your worries, your IVs, your planning, your replaying, your fast-forwarding—if you can take that weakness and say, "Lord, use it," you'll be astonished by what He will do.

OTHER TYPES OF DEVASTATION

Maybe your thing isn't cancer. Maybe your gut punch is something different. A devastating job loss. An unfaithful spouse. A chronically sick child. An injury that hasn't healed. Maybe you're afraid of the scary thing. Or maybe you're in it right now.

Whatever it is, take comfort in the Word of God, and know that whatever scary thing you're in or will be in, Jesus says that fear cannot defeat you. Cancer can wither a body and make it weak, but a strong God can shine brightly in you, even if it's by your death unlocking everlasting life.

My mom has already survived cancer. And my moment with cancer was a passing shadow. But I have a sweet friend, a young mom in Miami, who is living with cancer right now. And I know others who have died of cancer. How it shakes out while we're here varies. Sometimes we live, sometimes we die, but for Christians it means life either way. So, I can't say this enough—we can feel the sad feelings, but we don't have to feel the hopeless ones.

Christians don't have to fear death, because for Christians, to die is gain. Our fragile, broken bodies die, but we can be peaceful knowing that for us, to die is to finally fully live. How amazing! We can take our troubles to God and He can rescue us—maybe from the circumstance, but definitely from the fear.

> I sought the LORD, and he answered me
> and rescued me from all my fears. (Ps. 34:4)

WORSE THAN CANCER

I have another friend back home in Miami whose mom was diagnosed with an incurable, degenerative disease.

My friend's mom's diagnosis came around the same time my own mom was diagnosed with cancer. I was still in the emotional floundering stages of it all, googling what "Stage Three" meant and talking on the phone with my sister for hours saying helpful things like, "Man . . . I just . . . wow . . ."

And I was telling my friend about the shock of it all and she said something that shifted my perspective a little.

She said, "At least your mom can get better. There's no cure for what my mom has. She is just going to get sicker and weaker until she dies."

And that shook me up. I try not to think about things like that. Because hopelessness isn't pretty. Even when it's a hopeless physical situation afflicting a Christian person.

Nobody wants to hear that the thing can't go away. Nobody wants to be faced with something that doesn't get better.

There are physical diseases that are worse than cancer. Incurable diseases, where death is light at the end of the tunnel because that's when the pain will stop.

But even worse than the "worse than cancer" diseases, is the spiritual reality that we are working with and shopping with and sipping coffee next to souls that are afflicted by the hopeless disease of their sin, and they haven't accepted the grace of God through the work of Christ on the cross. We're bumping into them on elevators and shooting the breeze with them in line at CVS, and they have a "they can't make it better" disease. The bad one. The worse-than-anything-else one. And we have their only hope on the tips of our tongues and hidden in our hearts. The Word of God, the gospel, that saves, that heals, that changes things. The love of Jesus that transformed us. And we know it's real because we've tasted and seen it ourselves.

And yet, often we're not sharing it. Because that is another thing to fear.

We're sometimes scared of the awkwardness. And avoid it as though we're scared the lost people might "infect" us. We forget that we're immune to death. We forget that sadness and pain and decay and trauma is a vapor. Life "appears for a little while, then vanishes" (James 4:14).

How bizarre and wonderful that God allows us to play a part in His mission, to have these small roles in leading people to the only One who can satisfy and calm their soul.

DID YOU SAY HEROIN?

I brought my girls over to a friend's house for a playdate the other day, and my friend was telling me about a woman she had spent the past few evenings visiting. She had been trying to help this family who was struggling physically and financially, and she was fairly certain that after the woman handed her baby off to her, she went in the next room and shot up heroin.

As she was telling me this story, I felt soooooo uncomfortable. I didn't even want to hear about it, much less help with it. I almost couldn't believe it, that not only had my friend been over there three nights that week, but she wanted to go back again to bring dinner the next day.

I made some sort of comment about how awesome I thought it was that she was willing to do this super hard thing . . . and her response convicted my heart so much.

She said, "It's not hard at all . . . I'm happy to go visit . . . I wish I could help her set her life on a different path, and I'm not sure what that looks like, but even if my role is just to go over and hold her baby and talk to her, I'm so happy to do it . . . it's not hard."

And the Lord reminded me that I was and still am, in many ways, just like that heroin addict. I was lost and hopeless and sinful and in desperate need of someone to step into my life and show me the way. Even now, even as a child of God, I sometimes forget how needy I am, how poor in spirit I am, how selfish and wickedly wired I can be when I take my eyes off the cross for even a second.

I love that the Lord uses His people, whether directly or indirectly, to remind us who we are and why we're here.

We can fearlessly love the sick and poor and needy because we are sick and poor and needy. We are them, but we've been healed and changed by love.

Remember how I told you about the time I was at the doctor's office to get a shot and I threw my baby sister to the needles? *"TAKE HER!"*

Well, just a handful of years later, I found myself in my first house with my first baby and I had a stomach bug. The kind where you're like, "I'm going to die—how can you feel like this and throw up this many times and live, and will my home ever be the same after this?"

My sister was going to come babysit that night, and I told her, between gags, that I had the stomach flu and thought I was going to die . . . and that I understood if she didn't want to come anymore.

About an hour later, she showed up at my door. I think Brandon answered, on his way out the door, and I looked at my sister, turned my head, and puked all over the floor and wall. And that baby Biscuit of mine put one foot in front of the other, walked into my den of stomach sickness, and she babysat my baby. And then spent the next three days feeling like she was going to die.

Who does that!

People who put the needs of others above their own, that's who.

"So whatever you wish that others would do to you, do also to them, for this is the Law and the Prophets." (Matt. 7:12 ESV)

For me, so much of learning to be like Christ has happened simply by being a recipient of love—getting to experience the gift of others sacrificing for me and my well-being. And I look at them like, *How* and *why* are you like this? And then Christ gets my attention and my selfishness is exposed and my fears don't hold up when I look at the great, sacrificial, otherworldly love He has for me. And my heart says, "Yes, yes, yes, Lord! I want this! I want You!"

John Piper wrote an article called "Does Fear Belong in the Christian's Life?" In it, he writes,

> We think we will be better Christians when we stop fearing—that may be quite false. We will be better Christians when we love God the more for his perfect love. The perfecting of love necessarily drives out fear, but the driving out of fear does not necessarily mean that love is being perfected. One may wish to be rid of fear in the same way he wants to be rid of a bad conscience and he may use all the same deceptive means to shed this discomfort (e.g., alcohol, drugs, or more commonly, the elimination of all the commands in the Bible to fear God and to love him with your whole heart. See Deuteronomy 10:12).[10]

When we pursue God, when we love God because we have been loved by God, and with our whole hearts because He gave His whole heart and more, our fears will be "necessarily" diminished and we'll be able to walk in the power of the Spirit and love this cancer-sick world—this world whose future really is scary without Jesus. Our fears are defeated. We have no need for it. Jesus has overcome cancer and He killed death. He swallowed the wrath and crushed the enemy.

Though we walk through the valley of sickness and disease and the shadow of death, we really do have nothing to fear.

Ultimately, because of the gospel and the resurrection we know is coming, we are immune. We are healed. We are loved.

> Then they cried out to the LORD in their trouble; he saved them from their distress. He sent his word and healed them; he rescued them from the Pit. Let them give thanks to the LORD for his faithful love and his wondrous works for all humanity. (Ps. 107:19–21)

STARING AT BULLS

I'll finish this chapter with something I wrote on my blog the day after my mother's first chemotherapy infusion:

Sometimes, you're getting group texts from your dad about how brave your mom is during her first chemo, and while you're looking at them, your baby falls out of her high chair onto her head, and you're at a restaurant trying to be cheerful for your sweet mother-in-law's birthday dinner, and you whisk your freshly injured baby into the waiting area and stand facing the painting on the wall so no one will see you crying. But you see that you're face-to-face with a painting of a guy standing in a field full of bulls.

And the painting makes you think of being a five-year-old flower girl at your mom's second wedding because her new husband—the guy that would adopt and love you as if you were his daughter by blood—would attend his own wedding with a major pectoral injury he got cutting horns off of a bull at the farm his family owned. This is the guy who married your mom. Your mom who is getting her first chemo treatment during the birthday party you're at right now. And your baby is still crying from her fall. Now she has a big red bump on her little fuzzy head. It happened on your watch.

Once you gather yourself enough to return to the table, your older kid wants to know why you're crying and you say, "Grown-up stuff, Baby. Eat your broccoli."

Finally, you're putting your baby to bed and your mom texts you that she's nauseated and you feel sick inside, imagining the worst, preparing for the future, trying to have hope while also trying not to get your hopes up.

Then, you have a moment where you feel sorry for yourself, which is immediately replaced by feeling guilty for being so selfish. You think about what your mom must be feeling. What your mother-in-law with the weepy daughter-in-law at her party must be feeling. And then you feel even worse.

And then, you remember that crazy worldview you have that shapes who you are. The belief that a dead man rose and will come back for you and your mom on a white horse (Revelation 19)—that He split seas (Exodus 14) and healed lepers (Luke 17) and created the universe from nothing (Genesis 1)—and you remember the times He healed you and answered impossible prayers and opened your eyes to His goodness and His sovereignty.

And you exhale.

And you smile.

And you text your mom pictures of your babies playing.

And include lots of emojis.

And you go to sleep and dream of dark things.

And wake up with fresh mercies.

We're going to be okay.

No matter what, guys, we're going to be okay.

Chapter Six

EXPLODING ORGANS

My flesh and my heart my fail, but God is
the strength of my heart, my portion forever. (Ps. 73:26)

I knew the doctor wasn't going to say everything was looking happy and healthy. I knew that simply clearing my
throat shouldn't set fire to my stomach. I knew that a pattern of "concerning blood work" probably didn't indicate a
belly full of kittens and butterflies.

But I hoped.

I was young. So young that my purse was shaped like an
electric guitar and I had a bleached hair stripe that changed
color every couple of weeks. Still working one of those
"not it" jobs, I was glad to leave work early for my doctor's

appointment, despite all the cryptic phone conversations I'd had with nurses.

Before I left, I had a few minutes of quiet at my desk. I used the time and the quiet to make promises to God that I'd break. I went through the motions of being faithful, all the while, saying in my heart, "God, You'd better fix this."

The last thing in my prayer journal that day was a scribbly psalm. I wrote the words I wanted my heart to believe: ". . . in God I trust, I will not be afraid . . ." (Ps. 56:11).

I hoped that by writing the words with my hand, the sentiment would transfer to my heart.

So with undercooked faith and every cell in my body full of fear, I tried to obey in an effort to win my Father's favor—taking the right steps, subconsciously attempting to manipulate Him into giving me the outcome I hoped for—a healthy pregnancy that would lead to that baby I'd prayed for.

I wondered if He would reward my efforts by "working all things together for my good" (Rom. 8:28), or what I thought would be my good.

You know, like, *Hey, God! Here I am, praying.*

But, not just praying. I'm super praying!

Hey, Lord, I'm writing Bible verses down!

Are You seeing this right now?

Wow, look how much I've written.

My hand is literally cramping.

Surely, God, I should be rewarded by not almost dying, and not losing my baby, and not waking up to multiple blood transfusions . . .

I hoped. I expected. I'd put in handwriting, after all.

But instead, I woke up to IV bags of strangers' blood dripping into my arm. And I couldn't sit up straight without holding a pillow over my stomach that had just been slashed by a frenzy of doctors and nurses after they ran my gurney into a room with blinding lights and scrubs and scalpels and face masks and an ominous voice behind me that said, "Just count backwards from ten . . ."

Scary, right?

Even though gurneys were flying and time was moving at warp speed as blood pooled in my abdomen, there was one moment in the chaos that everything slowed down. I'd just been wheeled into the operating room. There were so many people in that room. They quickly moved me from the hospital bed to the operating table with a "One . . . two . . . three . . ." *shloop*, and then they all started touching me and hurrying around me with metal instruments.

The anesthesiologist was behind me, I think. He was pretty calm. As they twisted my arms around and got me situated, he noticed the tattoo on my wrist that reads "2 Cor. 5:17."

"What's the tattoo?" he said.

"If anyone is in Christ, he is a new creation . . ." I started, panting through pain and chattering teeth, "the old has passed away . . . see . . . the new has come . . ."

Did you know that when your body is going into hypovolemic shock, you feel extremely cold? Like shivering, five warmed hospital blankets are useless, Arctic Ocean swim type cold?

"Okay," he said, "Now, just relax and count backwards . . ."

I know he wasn't *trying* to sound creepy.

The pain and the DNR paperwork and the masks and needles and Brandon's worried face as I was being carted away weren't scary, in the moment. I was hurting so much, I truly would have welcomed a chain saw operated by spiders with no experience if I knew it was going to make the pain go away.

What I feared, laying on that table, wasn't the actual medical emergency I was experiencing, it was the status of my soul.

Do you know what I said to God, when I knew I only had five to ten more conscious seconds maybe ever to live my life?

I said, "If I should die before I wake, I pray the Lord my soul to take . . ."

Just typing that out crushes me.

The heart behind those words was, *Did I do it right? Do you love me, God? If I did it wrong, will you please take me anyway? I may not have been a good and faithful servant . . . can You still love me anyway?*

A desperate and panicked S.O.S. prayer from a children's rhyme.

I had been immersed in God's Word for a lifetime already. I'd been earnestly seeking Him for seasons of my life, and yet, I was still afraid to see Him. I was still afraid I might *not* ever see Him. I was still unsure of my faith. I doubted that I was His, in what could have been my last moments. I still thought His love for me was dependent on my good works. *Have I done enough to die right now?*

My dying self was so scared that I'd missed the mark, that my last words were a childhood poem, asking God to please take my soul . . . you know, if I didn't ask Him in precisely the right way all those other times.

It's just crazy to me, when I think about being wheeled back for that life-saving surgery in 2010 compared to being wheeled back for the "cancer baby" a few years later. The two experiences were so strikingly different. After the 2010 ectopic rupture, I woke up sad, angry, confused and distant from God.

With the "cancer baby," on the other hand, I woke up joyous and eager to be a mouthpiece for the gospel to spread into the far corners of my extended family.

So, what changed? What was different the second trag-edy around? The difference was my understanding of faith. The first time I was struggling to trust the strength of my faith. The second time I had learned to trust the strength of the Object of my faith.

NOT MY MIRACLE

After almost a week in the hospital bed on the heels of the tragedy, I found myself home, unable to go to work, and barely able to move. And there was my bedside table. And there was that prayer journal I'd diligently scribbled God's Word into just a week before my organs ruptured and my world imploded.

. . . in God I trust, I will not be afraid . . .
(Ps. 56:11)

It's true. I wasn't afraid in that moment. Instead, I was angry. I was numb. I was done.

Nothing was making sense to me.

Pain-stricken and myopic, I felt betrayed by the God I'd trusted to save me and lead me and love me.

Yeah, I knew Christians weren't promised easy lives. And I knew Jesus told His followers that they would suffer, but this kind of suffering wasn't making sense to me. You see, I'd prayed for this baby. I wasn't even a kid person. I didn't spend my childhood years babysitting and pining for a family of my own. In fact, I didn't really want to have kids when I found out having kids was painful and sometimes dangerous. As a little girl, I remember telling my grandma that having children just wasn't for me. Better safe than sorry.

But God had saved me. He had healed me. He was changing me. I was twenty-four and spending free time in His Word, and He was sanding away my fears and sinful tendencies, one rough spot at a time. And, one day, I thought, *I could be a mother. Maybe it's worth the risk.* So, I prayed that God would give me a daughter, and if He wouldn't mind, could it please happen before Christmas so I could tell my mom and sister, who lived in LA at the time, in person.

Then, just like magic, a positive pre-Christmas pregnancy test! A baby registry! A frantic search for nearby OB/GYNs.

And then, blood work that needed to be checked and rechecked. And numbers that meant things on papers that didn't look right. And the pain. My goodness, who knew pain like that existed?

But, hey. I knew God. He is in the business of doing miracles! I mean, look at what He'd already done in my life. Surely, this was part of some master plan of His to astound doctors and this Godsend-of-a-baby would be this tiny miracle that would lead people to Him, and I could rejoice and throw up my hands and say, "Look at what God has done! Look at this miracle! Trust God and believe! He is good and He is faithful and He brings dead things to life!"

But the big miracle I'd planned wasn't at all what God planned.

During that time, that phase in my life, I'd describe myself as a geriatric baby Christian. I'd lived a long, full life within the walls of Baptist community, but I was only starting to learn I REALLY needed a Savior.

So, though I loved God, I was still in the process of working out my "salvation with fear and trembling" (Phil. 2:12).

I was still battling my "am I good enough" mentality. Even when I lacked pinpointable phobias, I lived with an underlying anxiety that I was doing this whole life all wrong.

And now I'd proven my shaky faith to myself with my desperate, dying, rhyme-y prayer.

PUTTING HATS AND EGGS IN THE WRONG PLACES

After the surgery, and after the somber nurses telling me I'd lost a baby and a body part, and after a week of hospital food, I got thrust back into my life. My home. Rhythms kept happening and I was outside of it all. And I got way too all-up-in-my-head.

I was mad at myself for trusting God to make it all okay, and I was mad at God for giving me what I prayed for and then taking it away under such horrible circumstances. And I was unsure of what I should be doing outside of remembering to breathe.

Before all the trauma, I was busy. Always running around. I always had somewhere to be and something to do. At the time, I was working at a Christian school as a 4th grade teacher. I'd stay after school for a half hour to grade papers and help kids add and subtract (even though I still count on my fingers), and then I'd speed home and work on my fiction novel titled *Crayon Shavings*, which I later changed to *Photos and Freak Shows*, which, thank heavens, never saw the light of a publishing house. I read books about the publishing industry and sent out exactly ten million email "query letters" in an attempt to get a literary agent.

I was also serving at the church my husband pastored and helping him lead a ministry. Our relationship had never known anything different. We met at a church we both worked at. That first church, the one we met and married in, was a small church, so serving together sometimes looked like burning sermons titled, "Papi, I'm Cold" onto CDs from an Acer laptop or hand-perforating three hundred bulletins in someone's guest bedroom during a Christmas party.

"But Brandon, I want to be with people at the Christmas party . . ."

"THESE BULLETINS AREN'T GOING TO PERFORATE THEMSELVES."

Just kidding. He would never say that. But I did do some mean perforating.

Anyway, after the hospital, sidelined from most of life, I had too much time to take stock. All the things I'd done in the past to stay busy became physically impossible. And though it was a slow learning process, I learned that I'd been hanging my hat in the wrong place. Putting my eggs in . . . the wrong basket? Something about ducks in a row? I don't know which cliché works best here, but I was doing something very wrong.

The gospel message, though, is always taking the focus off our striving, off our self-prescribing, off our efforts and failures, and putting our focus where it belongs—on the cross, where Jesus' efforts and Jesus' victory became ours. God wants us to love Him in response to His great love for us. He wants us to know His striving IS our striving. As we get this, as we walk with Him, in love and in worship, the fear naturally lessens as our perspective naturally shifts off the brokenness in us and onto the goodness in Him. If we die before we wake, He will 100% take us because 100 percent of Christ's righteousness has been given to us.

When we hang our hats or put our eggs and ducks in the appropriate place (on the love of our Father) rather than running to Him for relief from the symptoms of a fleshy heart, He helps us feel the newness He's already given us. He really does. The Bible proclaims it and I have the following Bible verse tattooed on my wrist because of how fully I've experienced that truth.

"Therefore, if anyone is in Christ, he is a new creation; the old has passed away, and see, the new has come!"

As we see the work of the cross more clearly, and live in light of who it says we are, our fears are as powerless as an off-brand diaper in the presence of an infant poopsplosion. Sorry for that analogy. I just spent the week with my baby nephew.

But when we can see the cross clearly, we remember that we have already been rescued from everything sad and scary. My pastor, Josh Howerton, says, our salvation is absolutely dependent on good works. Just not ours.

That's everything. Really.

So if you find yourself counting backward from ten on a hospital gurney, if you feel an internal organ exploding, or if your flesh is failing in any way, you can still sleep in peace, because in Jesus, your soul is safe (Ps. 4:8).

If we're busy resting in God when the scary things in life happen to us, our knee-jerk fear responses will be replaced by supernatural peace. And it's simply a gift that comes as a chain reaction to being rooted in a finished work and knowing that God has already been bigger than the scary things.

A MOTHER-IN-LAW'S TEARS

When I got home from a week at the hospital, a week of blood transfusions, and practicing sitting up and puttering up and down hospital hallways, my husband carried me to our bed and gently tucked me in and went back to his life. He had to go back to work. And there was my Bible. Right on the nightstand where I'd left it.

I picked it up and the journal I'd written in and opened them, skimming over God's promises and my promises only to shut them right back up and slam them back down with just enough force to make a statement.

I looked away and said the first prayer I'd prayed since before my fallopian tube ruptured and my baby died and the last prayer I'd say for two months.

"God, I don't know what to say to You."

I'm so thankful that God isn't rattled when our faith is weak. When we're faithless, He is faithful. When we're selfish, He is selfless. He doesn't turn away when we tell Him of our hurt or our anger or the losses we don't understand. Our feelings don't change His feelings.

During that dark season, in the aftermath of the scary thing, I was a mess that kept getting messier. After a few months of bedridden TV addiction, I found myself back at work, newly in Christian counseling, reluctantly on anxiety pills, decidedly withdrawn, and still giving God the silent treatment.

My in-laws came to help us and feed us for a week in the aftermath. And God loved me through them so much, but I was too upset to really let it comfort me. My father-in-law scrubbed my kitchen linoleum on his hands and knees and it never before (or again) sparkled like it did that week. My mother-in-law brought trays of snacks to my bed, folded my laundry, and even offered to bathe me.

But one of the greatest, most supernatural moments of love I experienced during the time that I was wallowing in darkness, was the moment my mother-in-law came into my bedroom to find me crying. I was so angry with God.

She could have said, "How dare you be angry with God." She could have said, "You can just try for another baby."

But she didn't do any of that.

Anger spilled out of me as tears, and I think I said, through clenched teeth, "I just don't understand why . . ."

And she grabbed my hands, hard, and her eyes met mine and she was angry, too. Not in the immature, selfish way I was. But in the *right* way. And as tears rolled down her cheeks, she said, "I don't either."

I couldn't see it then, the love of my people and how God was using those people to get my eyes back on Him, but as I stewed and drifted further and further from Him, He continued to pursue me through the love and service and tears of His people.

YELL AT HIM

At the time, I was working at a Christian school. I sat in the office of a superior one day and numbly told her how long it had been since I prayed, expecting Christian platitudes or maybe even a slap on the wrist. But her answer surprised me.

"I told God I hated Him once," she said.

I was too depressed to react, but that shocked me.

"He knows how you're feeling. He knows you're weak. And He loves you anyway. Even when we change, He doesn't. You're angry. Go home and get alone and tell Him you're angry. And then, ask Him to speak to you, and then listen and see what He says back."

"I'm not angry . . . I just don't want to talk to Him."

"No, you are definitely angry," she said. "Go home, sit in a closet and talk to Him and tell Him the truth that you're afraid to even tell yourself. Tell Him anything you want. Yell at Him, even. He's strong enough. He wants to love you and you're giving Him the silent treatment. You need to open back up the lines of communication."

I have to tell you, I didn't sit in a closet that day.

And I actually never read the Christian book she sent home with me.

But her words rattled around in the back of my head for a few days. And I had other people giving me words of truth—directing me to David's emotions in the Psalms, his honest and open dialogue with God. But I was stubborn.

You know what got me back on speaking terms with God? A coffee date.

After a few months, I gave socializing a few attempts and went out with a friend I knew wouldn't judge me for letting despair take residence in me for so long.

My soy latte was the perfect temperature, warm and comforting, and my friend's face was accepting and kind. I asked her for life updates, and she leaned forward with a grin and launched into a story about dark things. Things that the Bible says the Lord hates.

I could feel my stomach turn and the Holy Spirit, who I'd crowded with so many falsely comforting feelings like self-pity and self-love and self-obsession, jolted me and I could barely breathe.

Well, this was new.

You see, I was still a pastor's wife. I was still a church-goer. Did I mention that I was a *pastor's wife* who wouldn't talk to God? I know we haven't talked about this much, but being a pastor's wife is a whole *thing*. My husband works for a Christian publisher now, so I'm usually viewed and spoken to, once again, like a normal member of society. But, when you are the pastor's wife, people speak to you more carefully. They use their pastor's wife appropriateness filter. If they do talk about sin in their life with you, it's with remorse and/or a hint of embarrassment. I was married to the pastor of the church and I worked at a Christian school, so there were no people calling me to revel in the details of an affair or crazy night they could barely remember.

But I got into my car after coffee that night and realized I'd become so distant from God, that this friend, who by the way was well aware of my "super extra holy" pastor's wife status, thought she could come to me and celebrate sin.

I had been so numb during that season, I don't think I cried much. But I pulled my car over that night because I couldn't see US-1 through the overflow of my tears that had been building up for months, and I could barely speak, but I leaned my head back and said, "God, I don't know if You're good anymore. But I know that I still want You. I don't want to live without You . . ."

Getting through that season was a process. It wasn't the lightning bolt change I'd experienced in the past. It was through people and prayer that I eventually limped back to the Lord and remembered that He is good, despite the evil and pain in this broken world.

One family at church told me, months later, that they'd spent three weeks praying and fasting for me. Who does that?

Now that I'm older and maybe wiser and a little more bruised up by the world than I once was, I look at younger ones walking through painful circumstances, and I almost want to shake them by the shoulders and beg them to talk to God. Cry your eyes out. Yell your feelings. Pray the Psalms.

David, as we've said, was an emotional basket case in his prayers. Sometimes he rejoiced and exalted the Lord. Sometimes he was consumed with worry and depression.

But he brought those feelings to the Lord. He didn't run from the Lord. And we can tell that the Psalms (written by David and others) are from people who felt pain intensely, while trusting the Lord.

It's interesting. Though there are some exceptions, I don't pick up a lot of God-directed anger in the Psalms. I think that means these writers had an appropriate view of God. They trusted that His ways really are higher than our ways (Isa. 55:9). They took their dark scary feelings to a huge, wise, sovereign God and were supernaturally comforted by Him.

LOWER FEELINGS, HIGHER WAYS

I love the example of this I see in Psalm 77:

> I cry aloud to God, aloud to God, and he will hear me. I sought the Lord in my day of trouble. My hands were continually lifted up all night long; I refused to be comforted. I think of God; I groan; I meditate; my spirit becomes weak. Selah. You have kept me from closing my eyes; I am troubled and cannot speak. I consider days of old, years long past. At night I remember my music; I meditate in my heart, and my spirit ponders. "Will the Lord reject me forever and never show favor? Is his promise at an end for all generations? Has God forgotten

to be gracious? Has he in anger withheld his compassion?" So I say, "I am grieved that the right hand of the Most High has changed." (vv. 1–10)

Isn't that crazy? Did you just see that? The writer is literally questioning God's character. "Has God forgotten to be gracious?" and then he quoted himself saying, 'I am grieved that the right hand of the Most High has changed."

This writer puts that in quotes, because it's not the truth. It's his feelings on a page. The Most High can't change, but our brains can wonder if He can.

I love the deep honesty in this psalm. Whoever wrote these words, inspired by God, was crying, groaning, suffering, QUESTIONING the Most High, most perfect, most definitely unchanging God. This writer is admittedly refusing to be comforted. Have you been there? I have; flip back a few pages.

Whoever wrote this was so troubled that at times he could not speak. And yet, he held onto the chance to talk to the Lord. He couldn't find answers, but he found a few weak words for the One who had the answers.

In verses 11–15, that same writer says, "I will remember the LORD's works; yes I will remember your ancient wonders. I will reflect on all you have done and meditate on your actions."

Get, ready, here it comes . . .

"God, your way is holy. What god is great like God? You are the God who works wonders; you revealed your strength among the peoples. With power you redeemed your people, the descendants of Jacob and Joseph. Selah"

Do you ever reflect back on the works and wonders of the Lord? Not just in the Bible, but in your own life? I'm frighteningly forgetful when it comes to remembering that God loves me and is for me and that He has already shown me in real ways in my own real life. This is why I love prayer-journaling so much.

I love keeping physical record of God's miracles and provisions and comforts. I love writing down how He makes a way when there was no way. You can see it in every page of the Bible and in every page of your own history, if you look.

The psalmist here in chapter 77 takes his frustration, his depression, his weak-minded questions, and mediates on the wonders and works of the Lord.

Pick up in verse 16: "The water saw you, God. The water saw you; it trembled. Even the depths shook. The clouds poured down water. The storm clouds thundered; your arrows flashed back and forth. The sound of your thunder was in the whirlwind; lightning lit up the world . . ." (vv. 16–18).

If you've ever spent an extended period of time in prayer, you can see what's happening in this writer's heart as he prays. He comes to the Lord confused and broken. He takes a moment to remember the works, wonders, and character of God, and the beauty of God breaks through to his heart. His thoughts shift away from his troubling circumstances and rest in the power of the God who makes the water tremble.

When well-meaning Christians quote "His ways are higher than our ways," it can absolutely sting a wounded heart, but it's the truth. And it doesn't sting so much when we rediscover it ourselves. His ways really are higher, and when we remember who He is, we remember that we can rest in Him down here in the lower places. We remember that He is Most High and that His Word isn't just a Band-Aid for small hurts. It is living and active. It lights our path. It points us to Jesus, whose death has already proven God's love, beyond question, regardless of what our circumstances may shout to us in our pain.

God used that dark season in my life to strengthen my faith and gift me with assurance of it. Through the actions of His people and the words of His book, He said, "I love you. I love you. I love you. I so loved you that I sent Jesus to carry your pain and heal your soul and give you everlasting hope and peace and overwhelming joy."

The Lord is so kind.

He was kind back then when I ran from Him in pain, and He was right there waiting when I hobbled back to Him in pieces.

He stood with open arms, ready for His broken daughter to return to Him with her stomach gash and her tears and her doubts. My months of anger and silence didn't blow my chance for His love. I was lamenting and He was still there, speaking in that still, small voice, saying, "For as the heaven is higher than the earth, so my ways are higher than your ways, and my thoughts than your thoughts . . ." (Isa. 55:9).

And also, I love you. I love you. I love you.

Psalm 34:19 says, "One who is righteous has many adversities, but the LORD rescues him from them all."

Second Corinthians 5:21 says, "He made the one who did not know sin to be sin for us, so that in him we might become the righteousness of God."

I think that puts us in a pretty good spot.

See, the Christian may visit, but we will never dwell in despair, because our fears have been defeated. "Scary" things lose their scariness (or, as 1 Corinthians 15:55 puts it, death loses its sting) when we remember that Jesus Himself, in John 16:33, told us that in this life we will have trouble, but we can take heart because He has overcome the world.

100 PERCENT FLESH FAILURE

We don't have to lay awake at night wondering if our flesh is going to fail us. Guys! It's totally going to. Look at history. Look at your grandparents. Look at the natural process of life. Flesh fails. Every time, it fails.

Not to get all scientific on you, but it's called entropy.

I just looked up "entropy" to make sure I had the right word and I could not understand even one word in the definition, but I'm pretty sure I'm right.

Everything we know and have experienced here on earth is decaying. That's entropy. My husband just preached at our church about this. He said the reality of entropy makes this verse ring true: "Even in laughter a heart may be sad, and joy may end in grief" (Prov. 14:13).

Even in our happy moments, there is an underlying sadness because we know that we and our people are temporary. We are falling apart. Our sweetest moments together with family or friends can't help but carry the not-so-secret burden than one day we won't all be together. Even the best moments in life are laced with the reality of death. This is unavoidable. But we don't have to fear it.

Our flesh may fail, but for the Christian, death isn't the end. It's an event. Because of the death of Another, it is truly the ultimate beginning.

Jesus' death on the cross purchased for us a future resurrected body that is renewed and entropy-proof and unfailing. His loving sacrifice ensured us access to God— access to cast our questions now and access to cast our crowns then. Because of Jesus, though I fail in my striving, though I fail in my diet plan, though my body fails me even when I have nothing to do with it, God is "the strength of my heart, my portion forever" (Ps. 73:26).

UNDEFEATED CHEER CHAMPION

I need to switch gears for a minute, because so far, this book doesn't have nearly enough cheerleading information in it. I was a cheerleader in high school. Not the pom-poms and "go team" kind, but the three hours of practice a day, taped-up wrists, crying and sweating and flipping and winning national competitions kind.

Being on the competition team was *serious*. It was my everything. And if I play out our first national championship winning routine in my mind from start to finish, and remember seeing Jen stick that last heel-stretch after having just landed my roundoff-backhandspring-backhandspring-tuck, I can easily trigger a full-blown weeping session of joy and nostalgia.

After I threw my biggest tumbling passes during competitions, if I really stuck the landing, I would turn to the judge's table with the biggest, fakest, open-mouth smile I could contort my face into while underlining the "DCS" on my chest with both hands.

I hate myself.

I joined the cheerleading team in 8th grade, and I didn't have a very good toe touch. A toe touch is that thing, when you jump and make your legs go straight out into a split, and you know it's a good one, if you can put your arms out parallel and your legs still extend over your arms, while staying straight.

Anyway, I wanted to be good at toe touching. So I would stand in front of the TV all day, the summer before ninth grade, perfecting my toe touch. I just did it over and over again all day.

One, two, clasp and squat and leap and touch and land and stand.

I wasn't the only cheerleader who took the sport seriously. Actually, the reason I took it so seriously was because the people around me took it that seriously.

During freshman year of high school, my fellow toe-touch-obsessed girls and I won first place in our division at Nationals. It was amazing. Then, it happened again the following year. Back-to-back champions. We were undefeated. We had trophies taller than we were and championship rings and an undeniable mastery of one of the least-transferable skill sets you can find on a high school campus.

But we were champions. It was intense. It was a dream come true. Two years into my high school career, I didn't know what it was like to be defeated.

And then, after two years of historic cheer glory, we lost.

The streak ended. We toe-touchers tasted defeat. And guess what? We never recovered. We were defeated and the team fell apart and we never won anything again.

Now, you probably weren't an over-zealous cheer champ (if you were though, let's talk), but I'm guessing you do know what it is like to lose. You know the ache of unmet expectations and the pain of broken dreams. You know the empty feeling of failure. Of failing family or friends. Of failing God.

We all find defeat. We lose sometimes. We fail. We feel hopeless. And sometimes we wonder.

We, little Christs, who carry the hope of the world inside of our chests, are tempted to believe the horrible lie that the sad and scary things we face can and will defeat us forever.

Lies.

Your fears will not defeat you; they can't—whatever they are.

They can't defeat you because whatever scary thing they represent has already been defeated by the all-powerful One when He walked out of His own grave.

We need to remind ourselves and we need to remind each other that we need Jesus and that we have Jesus and so the only losing that matters now is the losing of our "old self." We need to remind each other that the only pursuit with a true and unshakable payoff is the pursuit of Christ. We need to remind each other that though our flesh may fail we can live like we will never lose because Jesus has defeated death on our behalf. Jump up, right now, and touch your toes.

WHERE HOPE IS

The other day I was homeschooling my big one. We were reading about Mary Magdalene when she saw the empty tomb. She was looking for the failure of the flesh of the most important man in history. She was looking for a dead Savior and dead hopes.

> But Mary stood outside the tomb, crying. As she was crying, she stooped to look into the tomb. She saw two angels in white

sitting where Jesus's body had been lying, one at the head and the other at the feet. They said to her, "Woman, why are you crying?"

"Because they've taken away my Lord," she told them, "and I don't know where they've put him." (John 20:11–13)

During the seasons in my life when I've felt hopeless, I often sound like Mary, here. I could say it this way: "This painful, unfair, scary world has taken away my hope, and I don't know where to find it . . ."

But it is always in the same place it was in John 20. My hope is with Jesus and He is alive.

Whether you're comfortably resting or breathing into paper bags today, your hope for peace is seated right now at the right hand of God, and is always interceding for you (Rom. 8:34). He looks on you with compassion through the eyes of a man who lived where you live.

On Sunday, my pastor suggested that most Christians sway one way or the other—either focusing on Christ's deity or His humanity. If we're fixated on His deity, forgetting His humanity, we view Him as mean and scary and disappointed in us. If we are fixated on His humanity, ignoring His deity, we lack the fear that produces reverence and humility.

But when we remember that Jesus is both fully God and fully man, we remember that He looks at us, battling our anxiety, whether our flesh is functioning fully or failing miserably, and He feels compassion and empathy for His people. Because He did this, remember? He felt pain, and on His way to the cross, He even asked for a way out of the horrific physical, psychological, and spiritual torture He was about to experience.

> Going a little farther, he fell face down and prayed, "My Father, if it is possible, let this cup pass from me. Yet not as I will, but as you will." (Matt. 26:39)

Jesus was scared.

But God didn't remove the pain or change the plan and Jesus didn't back away. Jesus suffered through the scary, painful circumstances that accomplished His purpose to save the world. He sweated blood, received nail-punctured hands, and was run through with a spear in the side. And it should have been a failure for the flesh. But instead it was a failure for fear. Because when He walked out of the grave, the hole in His side and the holes in His hands only proved how completely He'd won. His blood wasn't wasted; it was bringing near all those who were formerly far off (Eph. 2:13).

What have we to fear? Jesus has already been broken for us and when He rose, He broke brokenness. Our fears cannot defeat us because everything we fear has only empty threats in light of the cross.

Organs explode. Bodies weaken. Pain comes.

So what? Jesus won. So even when our flesh fails us fully, we'll be fine. Because, guess what? If we should die before we wake, we know our souls the Lord will take.

Section 3

MY FEARS AREN'T FOREVER

Chapter Seven

THE MATRON OF HONOR TOAST

• • •• • • • • • • • • •• • •• • •

My sister asked me to give the matron of honor speech
at her wedding last spring and I was terrified. I was
nervous because I hadn't given any speech of any kind
since running for class president in sixth grade.

Hello, seventy-four middle schoolers I have known inti-
mately since I was five years old. My name, as you know, is
Scarlet Elizabeth Wessel, and I'm here to tell you how I can
change your life if you vote for me as class president. What is it
that you're hoping for this year? Miniature vending machines
in every locker? A giant swimming pool in the middle of the
parking lot? (Long pause for expected laughter that never
came because those aren't jokes and I wasn't funny.) Anyway,
I think you should vote for me . . . now let me conclude with
my rendition of Amy Grant's hit, "I Will Be Your Friend."
You can always depend on-a-me, I buh-lieve, until foreva

ends, I will be your friend, 'cause I'm neva gonna walk away, if the walls-a-come-a-down-some-ah-day . . .

Actually, the song wasn't part of the speech. The song was what I sang from a microphone during our sixth grade graduation.

My singing in front of friends went only a little better than my stumping in front of friends. Also, I only had two friends.

So, that was my full speech-making history for the first thirty years of my life and that made the idea of giving the matron of honor toast scary. However, adding to the trepidation was my very consistent track record of panicking under pressure when in front of people, regardless of the situation.

In tenth grade, I made All American for cheerleading, so I got to do an individual routine at cheer camp in front of hundreds of people. I had a solid routine. My music even had sound effects with coordinating dance moves. Like a "wa-pow" where I'd throw a punch and a bell ding where I'd do a toe-touch back-handspring. It was good. But as soon as I stood in front of the crowd, I blanked out, gave into my internal hysteria, and ran off the stage crying, smearing All-American-routine amounts of mascara with the back of my black spandex sleeve.

So, about this wedding toast.

I had what I wanted to say in my brain, but I didn't know what my body would do while standing in front of 150 people with a microphone. So I practiced for weeks. I talked to myself in the car and in the shower. I made notes on my phone.

My sister was going to have an outdoor wedding on some beautiful property her friends owned in Tennessee and the reception was supposed to take place in a barn. But on her big day, the clouds were dark, and we dug out our umbrellas and hid under the shelter of the barn, watching the sky unleash a monsoon on all the white wedding decorations we'd set up during the rehearsal the day before.

My sister and I and the rest of the bridal party, along with all the attendees willing to attempt an outdoor wedding in a deluge, hunkered down and posed for pictures in the barn while the less done-up men moved what could be salvaged into the charming barn.

The barn performed beautifully and Aubrey's wedding was dreamy under the twinkle lights. There was wood everywhere and bridesmaids in muted colors and the sound of rain hitting the barn roof in a way that felt just right.

I got caught up in all the love and was fully present and worry-free during the actual ceremony. I was so entranced that I forgot to straighten my sister's train once, but MoMo stepped in and did what had to be done.

But the speech wouldn't be avoided forever. And after the kiss and the claps and the catering, I kept my notes app open on my phone as my dad finished his toast, by tapping my screen over and over so it wouldn't disappear. It was going to be fine. But somehow (the world is broken, all is vanity, and one day everything will end in fire), twenty seconds before I took the mic, my incessant screen-touching erased my notes. They were gone. The mic was in hand, the notes were lost forever, and I was feverishly fighting the odd urge to fall back on a chorus from Amy Grant.

But, by what I'll call divine intervention, my toast was a hit. By that I mean I didn't blank out, panic, and/or run off the stage sobbing, and the people who have to tell me they loved it told me they loved it. So, a hit.

Hey, guys! I don't run off sobbing when I have to do something in front of a crowd like I did two decades ago.

It was a relief. It was a new feeling. Change had come. I'm not the same as I was when I was twelve. You probably aren't either, and we are different in ways that matter a lot more than matron of honor speeches.

That is because God is constantly in the beautiful business of making me new.

> Therefore, if anyone is in Christ, he is a new
> creation. The old has passed away; behold,
> the new has come. (2 Cor. 5:17)

We feel the back and forth of this almost daily. We hope to be "mature" in our faith, and yet, like Paul in Romans 7, we keep doing what we hate, and what we want to do, we don't do. Listen, I'm writing this book about anxiety, but I still battle my flesh, my fears, and propensity to panic.

I still sometimes fixate on the troubling and soul crushing, which drives my attention away from the One who holds the hope, the One who holds my heart, the One who is making me new. I fix my eyes on what is seen, and when I do, I suffer again.

> So we do not focus on what is seen, but on
> what is unseen. For what is seen is temporary,
> but what is unseen is eternal. (2 Cor. 4:18)

My moments of dependence on God in the midst of screaming children and laundry piles so large they offend me and writing deadlines that loom—while other children and other life responsibilities clamor for my attention—can quickly turn to pride, which turns to despair, which reminds me once again that I was made for dependence on Jesus.

I always, every time, again and again, find rest and freedom from fear in the arms God, but I still inhabit this broken body in this broken world.

I'm still afraid sometimes. And I bet you are, too. But we don't have to live in fear anymore.

Now, when I'm afraid, I'm afraid while knowing I won't *always* be afraid.

I will be made new. My fears are not forever.

LOUD LIVES, QUIET SOULS

Do you tend to look backward or forward when you feel afraid? Maybe you're like me. My fear from years past will keep me from fruitful things now. Maybe you had a bad experience as a teenager or perhaps you tried to serve a teenager once and it didn't go well. And so now, when you see a need in a teen's life, you look the other way. Your past fear is keeping you from being used by God.

Or maybe, and I think this is extremely common, your "what if" fear of future uncomfortable-ness or conflict keeps you from being a tool of the Lord. Maybe you want to invite your next-door neighbors over for dinner, but *what if* they say no and you feel weird? Or, *what if* they say yes and they ARE weird? What if inviting new people into your life means a little more dying to self than you're willing to do?

That stings so much to me. I wasted many days and months and years withholding love I have in me to give because I was afraid of what it would cost me. I was afraid it would cost me comfort and freedom and peace.

That's the lie the not-yet-new part of our hearts want us to believe. The lie is that the more isolated and "in control" we are, the more peace we'll feel. But actually, it's the opposite.

Isolation and "control" might produce a quieter life. But peace isn't a quiet life; peace is a quiet soul. Peace is the gift of Jesus through the work of Jesus that we can have no matter what's going on in our living rooms or our in-boxes or our Facebook feeds. The loudest of lives can't overwhelm the quiet that comes from Christ.

We have a peace that is not our own. We face fears that can't last forever. So just because we felt like our old self yesterday or an hour ago, it doesn't mean our fear has to dictate what we do today.

We can love others boldly—in a way that says, "Come on in. You're welcome here. Even if you are weird."

People who are able to live their days like that, with open arms and love that crowds out fear, are happy, joyful, peaceful people.

PRIDE IS A FREQUENT VISITOR

When we first brought Joy home, I remember texting the "Big Fam" (the group text with Brandon's side of the family) about how God had given me eternal perspective and peace even though Dewy and Joy had both been screaming and pooping all day. There were a few months in there when both were in diapers at the same time. I vaguely remember it being awful and I have repressed most of the details, while holding onto the miraculous moments of mercy God gifted me with during that time. So, there really were amazing moments of eternal perspective. But just a few hours after I sent that Big Fam text, I handed the kids to Brandon, locked myself in the bathroom, and threw my deodorant against the wall. It wasn't the deodorant's fault. Not my best moment.

Back and forth.

Old and new.

I struggle with fear and sin, and then I don't! I string a few days together when my thoughts lean upward and my hands are being used to love others rather than wringing themselves into a frenzy. And when that happens, almost every time and almost right away, I try to take credit. It might not be something I say out loud, but it's in my heart. As soon as the Lord uses me, I think to myself, *Well, now look-e-here! I'm getting so many points right now!*

And then I throw my deodorant against the wall and I'm like, Whoa, whoa, whoa, whoa. Where did that come from? I was doing SO WELL and that was new deodorant.

> If we say, "We have no sin," we are deceiving ourselves, and the truth is not in us. If we confess our sins, he is faithful and righteous to forgive us our sins and to cleanse us from all unrighteousness. (1 John 1:8–9)

I cycle through my weakness and see my sin and it consistently brings me back to the feet of Jesus. I mean, it's all the time. I rest in God's love, but I congratulate myself for resting and then I stop resting. The Spirit helps me see it. And He brings me back. Because He's refining me.

When I first became a Christian, I could spend weeks, and months, and probably years even, believing dangerous lies about myself—believing I could do something in my own strength. Believing I was entitled to the blessings I wanted. Believing I had Jesus, but probably didn't need Him.

You're probably the same way, even if you don't realize it.

We won't always get life right, you guys. We are weak and needy every day and we need to remember that every day. And we need to depend on God every day. That means we need the gospel every day, because the gospel says that we have both every-moment-weakness and every-moment-mercies.

> Because of the LORD's faithful love we do
> not perish, for his mercies never end. They
> are new every morning; great is your faith-
> fulness! (Lam. 3:22–23)

We're being made new, every morning, every minute by the already-and-not-yet work of Jesus. The work of Christ on the cross has ALREADY saved us and WILL save us forever. We are ALREADY new creations and we WILL BE new creations in a new kingdom for happily-ever-after.

So fear is still here, but it is defeated. There are still things in the not-yet that look like worries, but they are really just make-believe.

I'm not the same girl who ran off the cheer stage sobbing. But that doesn't mean I'll never cry again. It doesn't mean I'll never again feel embarrassment or fear.

We don't have to live in defeat over our past failures because we are new and we certainly don't have to live in fear over our future ones because we will be more new.

> And we all, with unveiled face, beholding
> the glory of the Lord, are being transformed
> into the same image from one degree of
> glory to another. For this comes from the
> Lord who is the Spirit. (2 Cor. 3:18 ESV)

We may not be as bright and shiny as we thought we were. But we are also not as bright and shiny as we will be. We're being made like Jesus, old to new, one degree at a time.

Maybe, like me, you lived under the weight of crippling fear in the past, but we don't have to *now*. God has promised that those who are in Christ are being made new now and will be fully made new in the future.

We can be peaceful inside because God keeps His promises and He is proving it every moment. And even when we don't feel peaceful inside, we can feel our fearing feelings with the understanding that our feelings will pass. And we can bring those feelings to the Lord, rather than running from Him, because our Jesus lived them. He is very well acquainted with sorrow (Isa. 53:3) and the scary that this world carries in it.

Jesus felt fear, but He didn't sin.

He didn't give into panic and let it keep Him from the grandest of grand sacrifices that has ever been. He didn't let the anticipation of carrying the weight of the world's sin on His own perfect body keep Him from the cross. No. He finished His prayer in the garden, "Yet not as I will, but as you will" (Matt. 26:39).

Christ's fear didn't paralyze Him, because—hello—He's God.

But your fear doesn't have to paralyze you either, because you can remember that—hello—Christ is in you, and so your fears are not forever.

You can remember that though you aren't God, you are God's.

REST AND THE HARDEST WORKER I KNOW

When I was little, I was often with Grandma Marlene, and she was often singing hymns and wiping her brow and carrying heavy furniture from one place to another. Always spiritedly cooking or finding all of the safety pins in the house and putting them into labeled Ziploc bags and other things like that.

She took care of me regularly when my mom worked after the divorce. I remember her propping me up on her lap in our kitchen with black and white tile and she'd sing, "She'll be comin' 'round the mountain when she comes, YEE-HAW!" and on every "Yee-Haw," I would grab her cheeks and stretch them out on the "Yee" and bring them back to their normal position on the "Haw." Yee-Haw!

Grandma has always, in every season I've known her, been so skilled at seeing the bright side of things. Every time I'd fill her in on elementary school drama or cheer-leading woes or homework misunderstandings, she sympathized and told me she remembered how hard it was to be young. But then, she'd talk about all the wonderful parts she remembered from being my age.

She spoke about trees and mountains with wonder and excitement and when I was at her house in Miami Shores, she'd sit outside with me for hours and push me in the hammock and sing, "I'm so happy and here's the reason why, Jesus took my burdens all awayyyy . . ." and I thought the lyrics were, "Jesus took my bird and saw away." I was troubled by this and wondered, *Why, Jesus? Why would You do that to my grandma? And why is she so happy about it?*

I'd continue chattering about my favorite subject—myself—and she'd listen and treat my problems like they were as big as I felt they were. And then, she'd always conclude by telling me she was thankful for her old age. She said she was thankful to be retired and slowing down in life.

And then she'd sing, "Darling, I am growing old, silver threads among the golllld . . ." She sang a lot.

I didn't see the important lessons she was teaching me then. I was more confused about the "bird and saw" lyrics and worried about whether or not there were any more vanilla wafers in her pantry. And as a wound-up-too-tight little girl, I thought to myself, *Wow . . . so when I'm old, THEN I can rest. Grandma must be so peaceful because she's old.*

But that wasn't it. She was peaceful because her mind wasn't set on her age or her husband's failing health or the other painful circumstances that drifted into and out of her life. Her mind was set on things above. So she found joy in being "old" as I'm sure she also found joy in being middle-aged and joy in being young.

> Set your minds on things above, not on earthly things. (Col. 3:2)

My grandma lived that way and continues to live that way now, even as a widow with a never-not-hurting knee, because she knows that the bad and scary and painful things that enter her life are not forever.

ANYTIME PEACE

I think there's a misconception, even for those of us speeding through the busy adulting years, that peace is something to look forward to or something left behind. It's something you had as a child and can't have again until you're retired and sipping a London Fog on a quiet porch somewhere in middle America.

But again, our hearts are wrong. I don't have to look forward to my twilight years for peace and tranquility. The Prince of Peace lives in me now. He has and is still making all things new, every minute of every day.

My daughter's classmate whose parents are divorced can be peaceful inside, even though her heart is split in two. Because the Prince of Peace lives in her.

My friend in her twenties, with two little boys, who is living in South Florida with terminal cancer, can be peaceful inside, because her boys have a heavenly Parent who adores them, and her eternity is secure.

The middle-aged mom with an empty nest and too much time on her hands who shops at my grocery store at the same time I do every week can rest as she prays for her children who keep forgetting to call her, because Jesus made her children and knows more about them than she ever could and He sees when they rise up and sit down and when they don't text back, and He sees that mom when she's lonely, and He knows how to love her like no other.

I can be peaceful when my unsaved family member who doesn't know the Prince of Peace crosses my mind and I wish he hadn't. I wish he hadn't because it makes me sad and afraid for him. When I am overwhelmed with sorrow over his soul and feeling hopeless for change, I can rest again in the sovereign God. Because "Jesus took my burdens all away . . ."

Our peace doesn't come from age or experience or what our relationship status is with our harder-to-love coworkers. Our peace comes from Jesus. Our peace stays because He stays.

FIGHTING FEAR WITH PROMISES

But, as I said, sometimes we are still afraid. I still wake up at 3 a.m. some nights, playing through the if-this-then-that scenarios that stress me out. I can't promise you that you'll always, in every moment, keep your eyes on Jesus and not on your circumstances, because you're a human. You're not perfect and you're not yet all-new.

Our hearts are prone to wander.

What I *can* promise you is that, as a child of God, you get all of forever after things you fear fade away.

James 4:14 says our lives are "like a vapor that appears for a little while, then vanishes."

Remembering that isn't pessimistic or morbid. It's magical. Our lives on Earth might be here today and gone tomorrow, but don't forget. We don't really pass away. Not really.

> "For God so loved the world, that he gave
> his only Son, that whoever believes in him
> should not perish but have eternal life."
> (John 3:16 ESV)

Have you ever considered the fact that Jesus died for you, but He didn't die for your fears? You will die for but a moment, and then enter into new life forever. But your fears will just die. It will be in eternity as though your fears have never been.

Maybe you picked this book up because you were doing better. You were feeling less afraid and less panicky, but then you backtracked. The thing that worked before isn't working now and you want a new thing that will last longer.

You need promises that last longer. You need a remedy rooted before the foundations of the world, confirmed by the sacrifice of God Himself, extending beyond the very concept of time. You can have a consistent hope that you will be fully healed and fully made new.

And don't think that only matters someday, after the vapor. Don't think, "We're all afraid! Life is scary! But hey, it's all good—someday, we'll all be dead!"

NO.

That's not it.

The gospel of Jesus and the promises of God in the Word of God work right now. Every one we read reminds us this is not the end. It cannot be the end. The promises are tied to God and He can have no end. Every promise that melts our heart and shapes how we see our world and our own self gives us strength to carry on and do what God has put us here to do—love the other scared people in this broken world.

We have promises.

If you're a person who breathes in the oxygen of a world that still suffers pain and death and evil, you need to write out the nailed-to-the-cross good news promises from God's Word and tape them on your bathroom mirror, and on the dashboard of your car, and pin them on your sleeve and glue them to the back of your favorite box of cereal. That's not sage wisdom from me. That's advice straight from the Bible.

Right after verse 5, "Love the LORD your God with all your heart, with all your soul, and with all your strength," Deuteronomy 6:6–9 says, "These words that I am giving you today are to be in your heart. Repeat them to your children. Talk about them when you sit in your house and when you walk along the road, when you lie down and when you get up. Bind them as a sign on your hand and let them be a symbol on your forehead. Write them on the doorposts of your house and on your city gates."

We can keep waking up everyday and taking our kids to school and folding laundry and sitting through meetings and standing in waiting rooms at doctors' offices, and we can take these true promises with us. We can talk about them and wear them and know them and remember them because when we do, we remember that our fears aren't forever. When we do, we remember Jesus is forever and we are forever and "there will be no more crying" is forever and "there will be no more mourning" is forever and "neither shall we hurt anymore" will be forever and nothing, nothing, nothing that causes tears or mourning or pain will be forever.

Please, get the back of your cereal box handy, and plaster these on it:

"I am sure of this, that he who started a good work in you will carry it on to completion until the day of Christ Jesus" (Phil. 1:6). God is sovereign and trustworthy and good. He will finish the job.

"I sought the LORD, and he answered me and delivered me from all my fears" (Ps. 34:4). I mean, goodness. Write this on your favorite child's face. Jesus hears me and delivers me from my fears.

"So we do not focus on what is seen, but what is unseen. For what is seen is temporary, but what is unseen is eternal" (2 Cor. 4:18). God is promising us that He and His kingdom are forever stuff. The bills and the medications and the parking tickets and the obituaries and the lawsuits are temporary.

"He gives strength to the faint and strengthens the powerless. Youths may become faint and weary, and young men stumble and fall, but those who trust in the LORD will renew their strength; they will soar on wings like eagles; they will run and not become weary, they will walk and not faint" (Isa. 40:29–31). This promise declares that our strength doesn't come from our youthfulness or health, but from the Lord.

"And my God will supply all your needs according to his riches in glory in Christ Jesus" (Phil. 4:19). You are God's, in Christ, and He has the riches of glory.

"For in my inner self I delight in God's law, but I see a different law in the parts of my body, waging war against the law of my mind and taking me prisoner to the law of sin in the parts of my body. What a wretched man I am! Who will rescue me from this body of death? Thanks be to God through Jesus Christ our Lord!" (Rom. 7:22–25). Some days we feel more old than we do new. Is there a promise that we will be rescued from this body of death? Who promises peace when our minds are at war? THANKS BE TO GOD THROUGH JESUS CHRIST OUR LORD!

LOOKING TO LINE UP WITH JESUS

One of the major things Jesus keeps teaching me about finding rest in Him is that I've got to look at the right thing. Sometimes it feels like just a matter of survival. I simply have to look up at Jesus, rather than outward and all around at the storm. I need to let my eyes linger on the words of the gospel, rather than the CT scan image or the troubling email.

The moments I'm looking at the right thing are the moments I feel the Holy Spirit transforming me.

So how can we chase these moments in life that might move us more and more into alignment with what Jesus says is true?

Well, I can tell you that God has used all kinds of different people and circumstances in my life to give direction and grow joy in my life.

Some of these conversations and circumstances have been larger than life—organs rupturing, fathers disappearing—the high-octane kind of trauma. But you know, most of these moments that seem to point me to Jesus—that remind me of His promises and help me line up more with who He says I am—start out as mundane as arranging blueberries on a sectioned toddler plate.

A BLUEBERRY MELTDOWN AND A KIND JESUS

A few months ago, I woke up and went to the kitchen while the girls were still asleep. When I got back, all three were in my bed. It made me smile. And we snuggled. And we did our morning things. And we went down for breakfast. And while I carefully arranged blueberries in the blueberry part of her pink sectioned plate, the two-year-old blonde started screaming at me, and I felt a familiar surge of panic so quickly it scared me.

And I realized, I already have a problem.

Why am I stressed and scared and taking deep breaths before seven a.m.? That screaming blonde is my treasured baby who makes me laugh and smile all day. Why does one second of her screaming make me feel so low? Why am I having such a hard time being and feeling calm and joyful right now when I have every reason to be calm and joyful right now? Why can't she just appreciate my berry placement?

And it clicked.

Side note: My husband had actually diagnosed the problem the night before, but what does he know? :)

Problem: I was never spending time ALONE with Jesus.

Never. I would write about Jesus at night and early in the morning while working on deadlines. And I'd talk to Him all day with my kids and read the Bible with them while I drank my coffee and I'd tell them what God said. And I'd been telling myself that was good. I'd been telling myself that was sufficient because that was the phase of life I was in at the moment.

At one point in my mothering, I'd had a "no one leaves their room until Mommy comes and gets them" policy, but bringing Joy home from China shook everything up. She needed easy access to us. And giving her sisters that access only seemed fair. I decided, then, that because there were always little kids around me, I needed to seek Jesus during the chaos. And I tried.

But that wasn't enough. Seeking Jesus in the chaos was good. Praying with my daughters is good. But my soul needed to be alone with Him. Just Him. Like, on a date.

So, after I put the breakfast on the table in a huff, I walked upstairs in a huff, and sat down in a huff, and tried to have "quiet time."

Except that it wasn't very quiet. The Holy Spirit's voice was so soft while the lies of my heart were so loud.

> **Spirit:** Scarlet . . . turn to the verse in Romans about Abraham's faith being counted to him as righteousness . . .

> **Scarlet:** SCARLET. YOU'RE THE WORST. TEXT YOUR HUSBAND ABOUT HOW MUCH YOU ARE THE WORST. OR GO MAKE THE GIRLS A BETTER BREAKFAST. GO DO SOMETHING.

> **Spirit:** Scarlet . . . you need Me.

And as I listened to the war of words in my head, God granted me grace to help me hear the still, small voice over the loud, scared one.

And I sat on my bed, fleeing the temptation to hate myself, to give in to fear, to obsess over the long list of things that disqualify me from being righteous, and I instead meditated on the true words of God. I had a moment to remember His promises.

I strained and I flipped pages and couldn't quite remember what it said in Romans about Abraham's faith being credited to him as righteousness.

And the Holy Spirit reminded me that I've been here before, and He guided my fingers to the verse, like it was a set of car keys I'd left in the same spot I always do, and I knew they were there all along.

And when God counted him as righteous, it wasn't just for Abraham's benefit. It was recorded for our benefit, too, assuring us that God will also count us as righteous if we believe in him, the one who raised Jesus our Lord from the dead. He was handed over to die because of our sins, and he was raised to life to make us right with God. (Rom. 4:23–25 NLT)

And immediately, the old, loud voice of Scarlet had no argument as I remembered again, for the thousandth time, that I am new. I am righteous because He is righteous. He whispered in the quiet that even in my absence, He is present. Even in my weakness, He is strong. Even in my anger, He is Love. Even when I won't be quiet, I am His and He is a single huff from having my heart. Sometimes I neglect Him, but He will never leave or forsake me. If I am faithless, He remains faithful, for He cannot deny Himself (2 Tim. 2:13).

And so I cried over what a terrible friend I'd been to Him and felt His arms wrapped around me, reminding me that He is, as always, the prodigal-loving God. He arranges all my blueberries while I cry at the world. I've been here so many times before, and as He held me on our little impromptu "date" that morning, I remembered that I am healed and clean and new already.

His voice was so loud in that moment. He was right there next to me, after all. And I didn't have to wait to get on His schedule or do some grand gesture to show Him how sorry I was.

I was just sorry. And He's just forgiving. And loving. And righteous. And true. And near. And for some insane reason, He loves me.

Preaching the promises of God, the ones you think you know backward and forward, can be a part of every day.

His Word, His promises, the hope He gives the hurting heart, put things into perspective.

• • • • •

I don't know when you had your last lightbulb experience with the Lord like my blueberry meltdown moment, but it's not something that we have to wait for or wish for. Because of the cross, we have true 24/7 access to the Father—to His forgiveness, His ear, His healing, His comfort and peace. We can communicate with Him any time and any place, but often we forget Him and we doubt Him and we seek comfort in the things we can see clearly, when all the glory of heaven is offered to us, here dimly, but someday, clear as day . . .

> For now we see in a mirror dimly, but then
> face to face . . ." (1 Cor. 13:12 ESV)

When I was a young adult, seeking and straining and striving to please God, His grace and mercy for me were harder for me to see. And I fought and stumbled along and fell on my face so many times.

Jesus extended His pierced hand and whispered, "Look at Me . . ."

Sometimes I tried.

I'd read His Words like they were made of gold.

And then other times, I forgot His Words and watched YouTube videos of people making their living doing funny voices.

But it might surprise you to learn that didn't satisfy my longing for peace and relationship.

So I went to Jesus again. And I was showered with grace again. And I was made aware of my sin yet again. And I begged the Father to forgive me, like I had so many times before. And, wonder of wonders, He always did.

And this learning and leaving and YouTubing and repenting and reexperiencing the wonder hasn't led me to keep sinning in the same ways. This hasn't pushed me to seek lesser pleasures.

This grace has led me closer and closer to the glass. It's made His face less dim and less dim each day. And I hope that at my last dying breath, my face is pushed so close to the glass that when I see my Shepherd face-to-face, He'll look almost just the way I'd always thought He might. I want to know I was looking closely.

I know you want it, too. And even if you think you don't, every single thing you chase for comfort is a lesser thing that He Himself created out of nothing. He is the source of all other joys.

Jesus Christ is the source of all calm. He is the Creator of comfort. He has defeated all the sad and scary things, so they can't harm you in the deepest ways. Your soul is secure. It is secure. Jesus is the thing—the One thing that you can hold onto when you're scared. He's who you can run to when you're feeling unhinged.

If you pay attention, you'll see His newness in your life, year after year, mercy after mercy, as He makes you like Him. I'm not who I was twenty years ago. Hey guys, I can give a wedding toast now! I bet, if given a chance today, I could finish a cheerleading routine without running off the stage sobbing. I may damage my ankles in irreparable ways, but I think I could do it without a mental breakdown.

I'm not who I was one year ago. Neither are you. There is freedom for us in falling short, because there is a future for us that won't fall short. Our Father made all things. And He is making all things new, pure, perfect, peaceful, complete, wonderful, beautiful, forever.

Chapter Eight

HOME AND SAFE AND LOVED

● ● ●● ●● ● ● ● ● ● ● ● ● ●● ● ●● ●● ●

When I was little, the closest thing I had to a security object was a furry platypus I named Googles. (This was before Google, the website, thank you.) Every day my SWAT-team dad would have Googles experiencing some sort of torture when I got home from school. Sometimes he was hanging from a string noose in my closet. Or he might have been closed in the laundry room double doors. Or smashed into the piano bench seat by one flipper. I've shared this, through laughter, with several people who, rather than laughing with me, looked a little disturbed for both me and Googles. I guess you had to be there.

When my firstborn, Ever, was one and a half, she bonded with "Boop"—a then-pink, now matted grayish-mauve stuffed lamb. Dewy took to a little fluffy dog she named, "Dee," but the family calls Dee, "Dewy's Boop."

You see, because of Boop's amazingness, "Boop" is no longer just a name, "Boop" is now an entire comfort species. I have several friends who have casually mentioned to me that their child needed to go get his or her "boop." It's really catching on. Trust me.

So, we bought some boop options for Joy before we went to China to go get her. A Chinese doll. A fluffy dog. A pink bunny.

Unfortunately, when we met Joy, she hated dolls. It was an instantaneous and deep dislike. As soon as she was presented any type of soft, fluffy and/or doll-shaped thing, she immediately swatted it away from her person.

"Get that Boop out of my face."

Instead of a bunny or a bear, pretty early on, she formed bonds with a miniature pink frisbee she got from the prize box at our dentist and a small blue pitcher.

I named them Fris-boop and Boop-itcher. They were the objects that gave Joy security during those early months in her new home. These objects never left her hands. Ever.

When we met Joy, all she owned was the outfit she had on and a little pink bow that looked like it had been torn off of some old orphanage toy. That first day with us, she held onto that bow and as many crackers and crumbs as she could keep in her little hands, but then we lost the bow. It was on day two, and we believe it got dropped in a Chinese grocery store, but we didn't feel capable of backtracking as we learned to be mobile with our three kids in tow.

It doesn't take a psychology degree to see that Joy clung to ratty bows and frisbees and pitchers and crumbs because she was afraid of being without. She was scared because she'd had more than just a small taste of this broken world.

SCARED OF ADOPTION

The year before we pursued adoption, I kept running into these cousins I never see. I mean, never. My dad grew up with six brothers and sisters and approximately one billion cousins. So, these particular cousins, I might have met three or four times ever. But because there happened to be two family weddings in my town in the same year, I kept bumping into them.

They're hard to miss. Since then, their family has grown even more, but when I double-bumped into them that year, they had three biological daughters and had recently brought two little girls with special needs from China into their family. They were kind and happy and had all five sisters wearing matching, embroidered dresses. And honestly, it made me feel very uncomfortable.

These cousins, my goodness, they are the kindest, most down-to-earth people you could imagine. But you see, their obedience to God, their unignorable "yes" to something so radical, a decision that required such fearlessness, reminded me of a thousand disobediences in my own life. Their willingness to be used by God exposed my own unwillingness. The picture of the gospel their family was displaying was in flashing neon lights. And I couldn't really identify if my life had even a chicken scratch, construction paper sign. Being next to them exposed that my fears often crippled me from being used, from being peaceful, from finding joy.

So I kind of avoided conversation with them. I wish I could say it was subconscious. But, like, I was actively avoiding them. I smiled and moved to other places in the building I "had to be." Like, don't I need to go check out the bathroom at this place? And was that my phone buzzing? No? Well, maybe the reception is bad in here. I better go check outside.

We left the wedding and life resumed.

Then, my other cousin got married and there they were again. This time, our table was near theirs. *How could they dare sit next to me with such a measly amount of fear?*

It was really striking, seeing their family function. Sweet sisters in matching dresses. I talked to my cousin's wife a little and she was so humble and real and sweet.

We became friends on Facebook.

It almost seems silly to say, but that friend request ended up having such an impact, that it may be one of the most significant clicks in my life of a million clicks.

Now, we were internet friends, and she posted a photo album and it said something like, "I know these photos are difficult to look at, but I feel the Lord might use them to lead someone to adopt."

And I clicked through photos of the orphanage where she picked up one of her daughters. There were dozens of cribs, lined up in rows, with nothing in them but plywood.

No mattresses. No blankets. The only soft material on any of the cribs were cloth ropes that were used to tie the kids' ankles to the cribs.

I can't remember whether I said something out loud about the Facebook photos or if my oldest daughter caught a glimpse of them over my shoulder, but a few days later, it came up while we were in the car.

"I'm so glad I have a mommy and a daddy," said my then-five-year-old, from the backseat.

"Me too, Baby."

"I'm so glad that I have a place to live and food to eat."

"Yep," I mumbled, trying to make a mental note to not forget the dishwasher detergent at the grocery store again.

"I'm so glad I don't have to live in one of those places with all the cribs and the wood and no mommy and daddy."

Wait. What?

Again, I really don't know whether she'd seen me looking at pictures my cousin posted on Facebook or if she heard me talking about it on the phone, but clearly she remembered.

And God used her words to move my heart toward adoption.

Adoption is something we talked about in our family for years. But our talks were mostly my husband saying, "I want to do this some day," and me flailing my arms out saying, "NOOOOOOOO! THAT'S NOT FOR MEEEEEEE."

Of course, I always thought adoption was a beautiful thing.

Remember, Paul Wessel, former SWAT, current doting grandfather, and all-around wonderful man, adopted me back when I was a bratty little five-year-old who really needed a good daddy.

You'd think that being adopted by Superman, and later by God Himself, would compel me to at least be open to adopting an orphan into my family. But see, I am *very* talented at shielding myself from uncomfortable things. I've had years of practice avoiding situations that scare me.

I was afraid of so many aspects of adoption. I was afraid of the form you had to fill out where you literally check "yes" or "no" or "may consider" boxes to things like race and gender and various special needs. I was afraid of choosing someone just like me and then feeling guilty for not choosing the child who was the most different, the most sick, the most needy. On the other hand, I was afraid of choosing the most different and the most sick and the most needy, because that's scary, too. I was afraid of what it would do to my family. I was afraid of what it would do to my marriage. I was afraid I wouldn't love the child enough. Or maybe I would love the child too much and give my other daughters a complex. I was afraid of adopting someone aggressive and angry and "unfixable." The list goes on . . .

OH NO, WE'RE ADOPTING

Brandon wanted to adopt for a long time, and I was resistant. In the five years leading up to the adoption decision, I'd had Baby #1 rupture an internal organ and almost kill me. I also had Baby #3 pretending to be cancer! And then, Baby #4, my little Dew, was the world's worst pregnancy. It was way worse than your pregnancy was. Cross my heart. What having kids did to me physically just had not been awesome, and I didn't want to talk about adding more of them, regardless of how they might arrive.

In fact, I got so tired of Brandon talking about adoption that I said, "Please don't bring this up for one year."

And he's great, so he really didn't. He just put a note on his calendar checklist for the following September 14th that said "Talk about adoption again."

But God loves Brandon and God loves orphans and God is powerful enough to soften the hardest hearts—the hearts that try to be made of bulletproof and fireproof and waterproof materials. The hearts that have an ADT alarm system, but not just a regular code, also a "duress code" specifically programmed for a situation where the heart might be held up at gunpoint and be told, "TELL ME YOUR CODE OR I'LL MAKE YOU STOP BEATING." But then the heart gives the gun-holder a "duress code" which makes the alarm turn off but signals the alarm company and police that there's a threat.

What? Stop looking at me like that.

God took care of it. He was working on my heart. Leading up to the conversation in the car with Ever, I was beginning to get creeped out by how many adoptive mothers were being put in my path like chess pieces in yoga pants. It was unnerving. Every woman I met, talked to, or

brushed past going to and from the grocery store and ballet class and soccer and church, had either adopted, was
in the process of adoption, or was thinking (and talking)
about adoption.

Then, this car conversation happened.

I responded the way I normally do.

"You know, Ever, it's a really beautiful thing when a
family has what they need to be able to adopt and give a
child a family and they want to do that. It's just like the
gospel. God adopted us into His family, making us His
daughters so that we can live in His house and be with
Him forever . . ."

I imagine God looked down at my silver Sentra roll-
ing over the speed bumps and smiled as He snapped His
fingers and exploded my heart. That's the only way I can
describe it. I was talking, He snapped His fingers, and my
heart exploded. I couldn't stop crying.

God moved mountains to pluck me out of hopelessness and make me His daughter. Jesus adjusted His life in
inconceivable ways to adopt me and give me "joy that is
inexpressible and filled with glory" (1 Pet. 1:8 ESV). In that
moment, God moved in my heart to want to give an orphan
a home and a family and a chance to hear the hope of Jesus.

I called Brandon as I drove our girls in the car and I
told him everything. He cried. I cried. We started the long
adoption process the next day.

What blows my mind is how God silenced every fear
I had. My love for an orphan I didn't know and the desire
to bring home a daughter was so strong that I didn't have

any brain space for the fears that plagued me before. All the questions and worries that I'd wrestled with in the past were gone instantaneously at the moment of the "God snap."

All the things I was afraid of—the special needs, the race and gender decisions, the potential personality problems, the questions of how it would affect me and mine—shifted. And rather than being caught up in how this sort of decision would affect me, I was caught up in the well-being of this child. This stranger. This kid I didn't even know.

How would her life change? How would food and shelter and the message of the gospel transform her future? How would God use me? How would He change our family to be more like Him? To care more about what He cares about? To hurt for what hurts Him?

Rather than worrying about picking someone "unfixable," God reminded me of the time He gave up every comfort and the glory of heaven itself to adopt me, maybe His most "unfixable" and definitely His most high-maintenance of creations. And He gave me love and food and shelter and Himself and a hope and a future.

Just typing it all out now is overwhelming. This is our inheritance. We, all of us, the scared and sinful and selfish have been given everything, not because of anything we did right, but because of what He did right. Because we are *so loved*. Because we are adopted.

THE BIBLE LIKES ADOPTION

Do you want to see how ALL OVER the Bible that truth is? Remembering and understanding this is one of the surest ways, not just to appreciate adoption, but to move away from fear. Remembering and understanding this reality takes scared people and makes them powerful people who live in the forever position they have been so radically given.

Read on and reflect on your adoption, finished by the death and resurrection of Christ . . .

> When the time came to completion, God sent his Son, born of a woman, born under the law, to redeem those under the law, so that we might receive adoption as sons. And because you are sons, God sent the Spirit of his Son into our hearts, crying, "Abba, Father!" So you are no longer a slave but a son, and if a son, then God has made you an heir. (Gal. 4:4–7)

> That is, it is not the children by physical descent who are God's children, but the children of the promise are considered to be the offspring. (Rom. 9:8)

> But to all who did receive him, he gave them the right to be children of God, to

those who believe in his name, who were born, not of natural descent, or of the will of flesh, or of the will of man, but of God. (John 1:12–13)

See what great love the Father has given us that we should be called God's children— and we are! (1 John 3:1)

For all those led by God's Spirit are God's sons. For you did not receive a spirit of slavery to fall back into fear. Instead, you received the Spirit of adoption, by whom we cry out, "Abba Father!" The Spirit himself testifies together with our spirit that we are God's children, and if children, also heirs—heirs of God and coheirs with Christ—if indeed we suffer with him so that we may also be glorified with him. For I consider that the sufferings of this present time are not worth comparing to the glory that is going to be revealed to us. (Rom. 8:14–18)

Even if my father and mother abandon me, the LORD cares for me. (Ps. 27:10)

. . . for through faith you are all sons of God in Christ Jesus. (Gal. 3:26)

He predestined us to be adopted as sons
through Jesus Christ for himself . . . (Eph.
1:5)

It's incredible.

Some of us didn't have parents. None of us have perfect
parents. No matter how good our earthly parents were, we
all have scars, we all have wounds, we all have needs no
human dad or mom can meet. But we've been adopted by
the one and only perfect Parent. By His own broken body,
He brought us into a forever family as literal princes and
princesses of the universe's only King. He will never abandon us or harm us or disown us or forget to pick us up from
school. He is never hard to reach or cold or petty. He is full
of grace and truth and He loves us with an everlasting love.

Maybe you had a good set of parents. Or maybe, like
Joy, you moved from homelessness in Tianjin to a town-
home in Tennessee.

Think about the safest you ever felt with your mom or
dad. For me, it was my mom's big bed. I remember that
on the days she wasn't working, she'd sleep in late, and
I'd crawl up into her Tiffany's colored puffy bed and we'd
snuggle up and we'd touch toes and I felt safe.

With God, we don't just get to *feel* safe. We're not just
enjoying the warmth of a mom and the refuge of a down
comforter wrapped over our shoulders. In Christ, we are
safe in the truest, deepest, and longest lasting sense.

In Christ, we can, as it says over and over in Hebrews
4, "enter the rest." We can trust, not only that He's out for

our good, but that He was willing to die the most horrible death to adopt and help us enter the rest.

THE SCARY DECISION CHECKLIST

When we entered into the adoption process, we received a zip file full of paperwork. I was like, "Wow, they said there was a lot of paperwork, but this is way more than a lot." And that zip file was probably one one-hundredth of the paperwork that was coming.

But, in that very first email from the adoption agency, we were told to fill out and return what was called a "Special Needs Consideration List." It was two and a half pages of ailments ranging from moles to autism to cancer and HIV/AIDS.

Brandon and I sat up in our bed that night and I read off the conditions and we answered in unison to each one. We were on the same page, mostly—saying no to the most "scary" sounding and yes to the most doable needs.

We felt good about our answers so far, but when we got to "deafness," I paused. One of us said, "I want to check yes to that." The other said, "I do, too. I don't know why. But I do."

I really don't remember who said it first, because the weird *hmm-is-this-something-we-could-pursue* moment happened for us at the same time.

So, we both agreed it was strange, but we checked yes. We sent it off and I got in the shower.

The shower is the place I have my most special prayers and also the place my fears can flourish. It's one of the only places and only times I'm truly alone with my thoughts—because THREE CHILDREN—and that time can go either way.

So I was washing my hair and thinking about special needs and starting to feel afraid. My initial "Yes" to deafness started feeling scary only a few minutes in. I thought, *Why in the world would we do this?*

I began praying out loud. I usually only pray out loud with my children or if I'm driving alone in the car and Nicole doesn't answer her phone. But, for whatever reason, I prayed out loud. I said, "God . . . why am I doing this? Deaf? Deafness? How even am I supposed to say that? Why would I ask my family to adjust their lives in such a dramatic way?"

And the Holy Spirit immediately answered, "Look how I adjusted My life for you."

And I did. I looked. I remembered. There was a cross and an adoption and Jesus checking "yes" in my story. I remembered, and remembering led to resting. And the peace flooded back in before I even dried my hair.

WHEN OUR FRIENDS LOVED THE FEAR OUT OF US

We say, all the time, that we never could have gone through with this call God gave us had the Deaf community not loved us so well.

After a few months of taking ASL classes at the local center for the Deaf and sitting in the corner at the local Deaf church, we finally had enough vocabulary to sign with one of the deacons that "We are Brandon and Scarlet and we're *maybe* adopting a three-year-old deaf girl from China."

The deacon then shared the news with the church and the whole congregation turned to us and gave what looked like gloriously excited spirit fingers. (That's how the Deaf culture applauds.) And then they prayed over us in sign language and they hugged us and we cried and it was just amazing.

Even though we were plugged into our home church, we continued attending the Deaf church a few Sundays a month leading up to Joy's "gotcha day." We just wanted to be around them. Seeing them love Jesus and love us made the whole concept of adopting our deaf daughter less terrifying.

The Deaf Christians there were loving and patient with us as we fumbled over our signs and said and did the wrong things on many occasions, I'm sure.

They gave us the sweetest send-off. The pastor signed all about our story and Joy's story and the whole church stood up and laid hands on us as they prayed for our trip in silence. My toddler was shrieking the whole time, but the prayer kept going. It didn't bother the Deaf members.

AFRAID IN CHINA

So, then we flew to China. We boarded a plane, all four of us, with as many tablets, headphones, travel books, and lollipop distractions as we could cram into a carry-on for the fourteen-hour flight.

Enduring that length of flight, with my two children who had never been on a plane, one of whom was two weeks from being two years old was something I assumed would be a traumatic horror story that I would repress immediately. But it wasn't so bad.

There were screens on the back of each seat that showed where our plane was on the map. We flew over the North Pole, you guys. It was crazy.

Everyone was Chinese. Really, everyone. There was a young, college-aged Chinese guy, translating what the confused woman sitting beside us was saying.

"Why are you going to Beijing? Why would you adopt someone? Is someone paying you to do this?"

We survived the flight and arrived in Beijing. We were so deliriously tired. It was like, *Good night! Or good morning! Or I don't know what day or time it is and who am I and is it time for the morning foods or the evening foods, and we eat rice either way, right?*

Everything was so different. The food. The city. The interactions with people. There was no time to be afraid.

But then we met Joy. And the fears I thought I was free from came roaring back.

It's hard to find words to describe the moment. When this person you've never met gets dropped in your lap. She's not a trusting newborn who fits into the crook of your arm with ease, like she's been taking up residence inside your body for most of a year.

It's different.

She's a stranger. She's lived a life. When she should have been fed, she was not. When she should have been held, she was suffering alone. When she should have been rocked and carried and touched, she was left in a crib for so long that her head is, and always will be, misshapen.

When she gets handed over, she doesn't look into your eyes and know that you are about to shelter her and love her and provide for her. She looks past your eyes. She leans away. She hits you in the face.

She's stiff. She's sad. She's scared.

It's a moment I thought we trained for like marathon runners. We read the required books. We watched the required videos. We filled out the required forms. We did our stretches. None of this was a surprise in my head. But it was a shock to my heart.

Pride is such a sneaky thing.

I glided through the adoption process high on my faith. God proved Himself trustworthy every day—through the amazing generosity of friends and strangers who helped provide what we needed to make this happen, through the almost-eerie opening of doors that led us to this specific little girl, through intimate moments with the Lord, speaking to my soul through His Word, as if He were right in the room with me.

I trusted Him. I know I did. But somewhere in there I started trusting me.

During our training, we learned about how difficult it would be in China. We learned about attachment and how hard it would be for the child, and how hard it could be, even for us. But I thought I would be fine. I knew I'd be fine. I mean, look at what God had done! I wasn't supposed to struggle. I've lost count of how many people I told, before getting on that plane, "Even if the details of this adoption end up a worst-case-scenario, I'm not afraid. God has been so faithful, how can I not trust whatever He has for us in this?"

And I meant it. I wasn't afraid. I knew things could be tough and I knew God could be trusted. I was as prepared as I thought I could be.

But then I got to China. And I was handed this girl.

This starving, severely developmentally delayed, fearful, flailing, tiny, earless deaf girl. I felt so much compassion for her, but I didn't feel ready.

And suddenly, I didn't feel okay. Suddenly, I *was* scared. Incredibly, crushingly scared.

I'd done the training, but truthfully, I hadn't really believed that the training applied to me. I'd subtly listened to the lie that "I'm strong enough. I'm better. I'm more equipped for this than the 'weaker' parents from the training who struggled."

My pride and judgment from the past few months leading up to the trip was instantly exposed to me, but repentance wasn't my first idea. Rather, my first ideas were isolation, ignoring texts from my friends, and despair.

We looked at Joy and saw what we thought might be a worst-case-scenario that we knew might be possible all along. That first week, she was an almost four-year-old who was the size of a one-year-old. She flailed constantly and couldn't seem to learn anything. And Brandon and I were convinced, for days, that we'd just adopted a child who would never grow, never learn, never communicate . . .

God gave us this girl. We knew that to be true. And we loved her already. But I spent those first days grieving. I grieved the simpler days of soccer practice and laughing in my home with my healthy, happy girls. I grieved the hopes I had of signing the gospel to Joy, so she could understand and know grace and freedom. I grieved for my plans to see her grow up and thrive.

And I was angry at myself for grieving. And angry at myself for being weak. Angry at myself for being afraid. Angry at myself for sinning. Angry.

How could I be so stupid? How could I be so proud? How did I think I was doing this with the Lord all those months, and look at me now? Look at how sad I am! Look at how stiff she is when I try to rock her. If I'd really been walking with God, I wouldn't feel so much fear and sadness right now! I'd be celebrating! Do I know my own heart?? Does the Lord know my heart? Is He going to take care of me?

The fear I thought was behind me welled up and I could barely function, let alone continue caring for myself and my family and this brand-new child in this strange new country.

Thank God for my husband who had the brilliant idea that maybe I needed to repent of pride. When he said that, sitting on the edge of the bed in China, it took me a minute to remember that repentance was a thing. It took me a minute to remember that the Holy Spirit intercedes for me.

So I buried my leaky mascara-smeared eyes into the white hotel comforter (sorry, room cleaner), and I told God I was so sorry and so prideful and so weak and so *scared*, and so in need of Him.

And under that blanket, there in Guangzhou, there really was a God who really heard my heart and really forgave me and really decided to shower me with grace, instant grace in that moment, in that hotel room, thousands and thousands of miles from home.

Later that day, Joy learned how to sign "food." And then she learned "drink." And now, almost a year in, she uses full sentences in sign language to say things like, "Can I have please Mommy water?" or "I don't like this celery." or "Cookie." or "Cookie, please." or "Cookie, again."

It's crazy.

At some point that week in China, when the future of our lives looked so scary, when I wondered if we'd ever laugh again or if life would always feel overwhelmingly heavy, I received a video compilation from all the women at the Deaf church back home, welcoming Joy home, signing things to her like, "Joy! We love you! We have prayed for you! We can't wait to teach you about Jesus! Your family loves you so much . . ."

I opened my suitcase to find clean socks and there was a Scripture card that my friend had given me to pack in my suitcase.

In the midst of fear and sadness and a situation that felt hopeless and sad, the body of Christ, the one I'm adopted into, held me together.

COMING HOME WITH JOY

Returning home, the jet lag was more insane than they even warn you it is. People say it's bad, and I was all, "Pish posh, I have Norwegian Viking blood." But the thing is, I was basically a dead person.

On day four or five back home, Brandon went back to work, and my body just shut down. It was my first day home with three daughters and no Brandon. I vaguely remember the day being full of blessings and love and moments that filled my heart with joy, but also I was physically exhausted.

I was emotionally wiped out, too. We all were. Brandon and I were trying to keep life chipper and chugging along, while wrestling with questions about Joy's future and well-being, and trying not to be overwhelmed by the fear.

At almost four years old, she could not communicate beyond signing food and drink, could not walk, and was not potty trained. Blood work and doctor visits revealed a host of additional unexpected issues, as well. And early on, it felt like we were all hanging on by a thread.

We were awake for about thirty hours on travel day, or "the double day," as I called it. And for the days that followed, I'd get two to four hours of sleep a night because thirteen-hour jet lag times five people taking turns being awake equals me not sleeping ever again. Or that's what it felt like that week, anyway.

Around four in the afternoon of the "why does Brandon have to have a job" day, I said to Ever, "I'm sorry, but I can't be conscious anymore. Will you please put the littles in front of a show and get them whatever they need and do whatever you all want? I just have to close my . . ."

And I fell asleep.

Somewhere in there, my phone dinged, but I was too tired to look at it. When I did, I saw that it was my friend Caroline texting to let me know dinner had been dropped at my doorstep. Not just any dinner, but homemade "Soup Noodle." She figured out how to make Joy's favorite food from China and left it hot and ready at my doorstep.

I stumbled down the stairs to retrieve it and passed my then-six-year-old who was putting dishes away without being asked to.

When I look back at that time, when everything felt uncertain and the only thing that did feel certain was that life was certainly scary, I am overcome with gratitude and joy. It was such a special time. Never before or again since did I feel so loved, so cared for, so prayed over, and so held together by the body of Christ.

We all live in this broken place, you guys. It's scary out here. We can't do it without each other. And the gifts that come from learning to lean on one another are priceless. Through my community, in the midst of such "scary," I was protected in a bubble of peace.

WHEN WE ACT LIKE ORPHANS

Joy's attachment to her pink frisbee and blue pitcher lasted for a few months, but the more secure she felt in our family, the less tightly she clung to them, and eventually, she forgot them completely. Early on, Joy would cry when I got out of the car and walked around to get her out of her car seat. She'd cry and look at me through the window, like she thought I wasn't going to get her out. Now, she signs to ask me where we're going and cheers with exuberance whenever I sign something she recognizes—store, Great-Grandma's house, YMCA. WHEE!!!!!!!

She is still growing and healing and learning what it means to be loved in a family, but it's truly striking to see her now and remember her then.

That's how it is with us, too.

We can look back at ourselves before we knew Jesus, before our adoption, and sigh in relief that we no longer feel the need to cling to blue pitchers and pink frisbees. It's something we can look back on with awe and gratitude, not something we need to look back on with shame and embarrassment.

Look down at your hands. Maybe you're picking at your nails like I am, but are you holding a blue pitcher or a pink frisbee? Probably not. Do you struggle with the same things you did ten years ago? Probably not, but even if you do, you know you don't have to now. You don't have to anymore. In Christ, we are free. The victory has already been won—by Him.

But yes we forget. I know so many people, myself included, who occasionally cling to blue pitchers and pink frisbees for security, because we don't fully understand what it means to be a son or a daughter. To have a home. To be in God's forever family.

It feels silly that I still battle insecurity, but I do. I so often find myself wiping mascara off my face *again*, re-explaining to my oldest, *again*, that Mommy's identity is in what Jesus accomplished on the cross, not what she accomplished today. That Mommy can rest and doesn't need to panic about not being on time or not finishing the thing she was trying to finish that day, because Jesus has already won the battle of good vs. evil.

It's such a gift to have lived with God long enough to know what it means to be His kid. To be able to run into His arms. To know that He's always coming to get me out of my car seat. To know that I don't need a third snack or a Boop-itcher or a Fris-boop because I have all I need in Him.

I don't know what your family vibe is right now. Mine has been a little nuts the past few years. We laugh a lot. We cry a lot. There is a lot of dancing, tickle fights, and dirty cheeks that get left that way when we leave the house because WHY EVEN TRY, THEY ARE ALWAYS DIRTY. The days are long and sweet and messy. And I know the tears and the messes aren't for nothing. The tears and the messes are lessons to my daughters and review lessons to me—that our security, our peace, our joy can't be found in money or relationships or frisbees or pitchers. We are God's kids, so we can laugh with empty hands.

LOVE IS HARD

Maybe you haven't recently adopted someone. Maybe your current challenge is your marriage, or your biological kids, or a boss you are trying SO HARD to respect. I don't know what it is for you, but loving and not fearing, even in light of Jesus, is NOT always easy. But sometimes it is.

I love it when love feels easy. Love felt really easy the day after I got engaged. Brandon and I were young and silly and our deep-rooted flaws were hidden behind makeup and electric guitars and comedy series binges.

Love didn't feel easy the first time we hit bumps in the road. After a few years of the shiny infatuation gloss wearing off, we looked at each other and realized, *Okay, loving this person is HARD right now.*

But, then something cool happened. Love grew through the hard and rooted deep into it. Like, man. I wouldn't trade the NOW love I have with my Brandon for the glossy kind we started out with for a second.

In one of his books, *The Meaning of Marriage,* Tim Keller writes, "To be loved but not known is comforting but superficial. To be known and not loved is our greatest fear. But to be fully known and truly loved is, well, a lot like being loved by God. It is what we need more than anything. It liberates us from pretense, humbles us out of our self-righteousness, and fortifies us for any difficulty life can throw at us."

Loving people through the hard times, through the hurts and the flaws and coming to the other side of it and seeing, "Wow! I am still loved and I still love this person!" THAT is the kind to treasure. That is the kind that is both rooted and shimmering, not like a cheap shiny gloss, but like a diamond. Did you know that a diamond has the highest hardness and thermal conductivity of any bulk material? I'm not sure exactly what that means, but diamonds are strong. And beautiful.

Love that doesn't *always* feel easy is the kind of love that will stop you in your tracks and change your life. Love like that drives out fear.

> There is no fear in love; instead, perfect love
> drives out fear. (1 John 4:18)

True love is challenging. It often requires yesses when everything in you wants to scream NO. It requires sacrifice when all you want to do is eat ice cream and lay in bed.

Nobody wants to think that they're hard to love, but guys, we are! If you think you're not hard to love, you're probably the worst. It's just true.

We are all so hard to love. Even when we're being our most lovable. We are forgetful and proud. We are so quick to take credit for what we do with these hands—hands that were fashioned for us by the all-powerful Creator. Hands that work because a bajillion cells are functioning within a system created by the most intelligent of designers. Humility is something we take credit for as soon as we notice we have it and then, poof, it's false. Our humility itself turns to pride.

We don't act like children secure in the love of our Father. So often, we act like orphans who are desperately looking for love.

We act like abandoned kids who are seeking the approval they didn't get from a parent through every word from our mouth and every post on our Instagram.

And all the while, we have the God of the universe constantly ready to reassure us, "Yes, child. You are so loved. Have you forgotten all the ways? Look back at My Word. Look back at your prayer journals. Look back in your memory and remember how loved you are."

JIM CARREY AND FULL TRUTHS

Adopting Joy is one of the best decisions Brandon and I ever made. Every day since we met her, there have been moments when this new calling—doing it fully and doing it well—have been hard. And I feel overly weak. Then, I open my mailbox to find cards from friends with perfect, anointed words of comfort and grace. Handwritten Scripture. Bouquets of flowers. And their love reminds me to renounce the lies. The lies that my not-enoughness is what matters.

Their love leads me into the love of Jesus, when I forget that I have it. Their love reminds me of the true love I can find and refine and experience through the Word of God.

When I forget, when I isolate myself, when I spend more time looking at the sad and the bad and the scary, I only remember half of the truth. I only remember that life is scary and that I am not enough. I remember that I'm weak and helpless in a world that's passing away.

I have so many needs. And He doesn't just meet them all. He is constantly flooring me with His intimate provisions and love and extravagant gifts—assurance of love in Him, joy in the midst of turmoil, peaceful sleep. Tell me what is better than that. There isn't anything else.

Look at what Jim Carrey, non-Christian, had-everything-else actor tweeted.

"I think everybody should get rich and famous and do everything they ever dreamed of so they can see that it's not the answer."

When I bring my fears and my weakness and my helplessness and my orphan-like tendencies to God's Word, I remember the FULL truth.

Full Truth: I am not enough. I am WAY too weak to love the people in my life sacrificially. I am way too weak even to be lovable myself. BUT . . . God's power is made perfect in weakness.

I'm not sure I've ever read anything more beautiful:

But he said to me, "My grace is sufficient for you, for my power is perfected in weakness." Therefore, I will most gladly boast all the more about my aweaknesses, so that Christ's power may reside in me. (2 Cor. 12:9)

YOU ARE HOME, YOU ARE SAFE, AND YOU ARE LOVED

I forget these truths all the time. Then, I remember them. I remember—*OH. Christ's power resides in me. I'm not helpless. I'm not really weak. I'm not, because I'm not me. I'm a Christian. I'm a "little Jesus."*

In Him and through Him, I have power to love and power to help and power to be selfless. I, really, even ME, have the power to be courageous.

All over the Old Testament, I read story after story of cowards being made courageous through the Spirit of God. Abraham. Moses. Gideon.

It's everywhere. The Bible doesn't exalt the Goliaths. It exalts the humble.

"Whoever exalts himself will be humbled, and whoever humbles himself will be exalted." (Matt. 23:12)

Just like my little Joy is learning how to live like she's part of the Hiltibidal family, I'm still learning to live like I'm in God's family. I'm still remembering and forgetting and reminding my children and being reminded by my friends that God, the author of love, is my adoptive Dad.

> God in his holy dwelling is a father of the
> fatherless and a champion of widows. God
> provides homes for those who are deserted.
> (Ps. 68:5–6)

Adoption has taught me so much, and it has been a blessing to our family in so many ways, but the greatest thing it's done in my heart has been to remind me, over and over again, Who has adopted me.

I still feel fear and I still feel frustration and I still sin and struggle, but waking up to the face of my adopted daughter each day reminds me of my adoption through Christ. And that reality brings me to peace.

It brings me right back to that spot of neediness, of desperation, of childlike, orphan-like dependence. And I inhale His goodness and exhale His love and relish His peace. And I wipe my happy and sad and tired and excited and frustrated tears away a million times a day and I keep going.

And I fight to switch over from "try to be good at life" and "try to be brave" to "Jesus is good to me" and "Jesus is strong for me." And I keep thanking Him.

We are not hopeless. Our fears are temporary. We are not lost. We are home. We are not forgotten. We are treasured.

Grace is ours. God is real. Joy is home and safe and loved. And so are we.

Chapter Nine

GRANDPA DIED—"THE FUNNEST DAY EVER"

• • • • • • • • • • • • • • • • • •

My grandpa died on a Tuesday in April.

Because of that, my family was sitting in the back of a van, driving around the graveyard while a guy named Paul (not my dad) told us which burial garden options were most expensive. Grandma was in the front, dazed, asking questions. My dad, my cheeto-scarfing-then-one-year-old and I took the middle row. My mom, sister, and my then-five-year-old were in the back-back. Joy wasn't on our radar yet.

As we drove by a giant carving of The Last Supper, my five-year-old said she was hungry from the back row, and my dad somberly responded, "Let's all go out to dinner after this. That okay, Scarlet?"

I nodded as my eyes scanned the headstones and heard my five-year-old from the seat behind me say a little too loudly and little too excitedly, "Dinner? At a restaurant??"

I nodded again, gravely, and looked in her direction. I tried to give her a "don't do what I think you are about to do" stare, but she'd heard the word "restaurant" and would not be held back.

Her skinny little arms shot up and her hands turned into fists, and in full outside-voice volume she shouted, "THIS IS THE FUNNEST DAY EVERRRRRR!!!!!!!!!!!!"

Yes, of course I see the humor in it now. But in the moment, my sister and I wore matching horrified faces, and bugged our eyes out at my five-year-old to communicate, "YOU DON'T SAY THAT THE DAY GRANDMA'S LOVE OF SIXTY YEARS DIED IS THE 'FUNNEST DAY EVER!' DON'T YOU KNOW THAT?!"

Then, we all lost it. Everyone. The whole car shook with laughter. My innocent five-year-old was oblivious to all reactions as she was still trembling with giddiness at the idea of eating at a restaurant.

And then, my dad said, "You're right, Ever. Grandpa is with Jesus right now. For him, this *is* the funnest day ever."

Crisis averted. Truth remembered.

THE DAY HE DIED

I didn't cry much when I got the text that afternoon—the day my grandpa had died. We'd all been expecting his death for a long time. He suffered horribly for years. But, of course, death itself is still a shock. You don't expect it, even when you think you're expecting it.

I had just finished Ever's ballet bun for picture day and was in the midst of the leave-the-house-checklist madness. Ballet shoes? Check. Change of clothes for everyone (that has its own sub-checklist)? Check. Baby cheetos/pouches/sippy cup? Check. Diapers? Check. Wipies? Check . . .

I was in an overly fantastic mood, texting my sister-in-law about something happy when I got the text from my mom. In fact, I might have been texting Lauren about our interest in adoption. Then, the text notification from my mom popped up over the text I was typing.

"Grandpa died. 11:20."

My daughter saw my tears, and when I told her Grandpa died, her face scrunched up and she said, "Why are you crying, Mommy? Isn't he in heaven now? Isn't that what you said?"

She got over the fact that we needed to skip ballet pictures pretty quickly, and we sped over to my grandma's house and walked in right as my grandma was shifting Grandpa's body around.

Nobody tells you about this part of death. Or, I never heard about it anyway. When people I didn't know that well died, we'd see them in a casket or hear about the event that took place when death happened. I had never thought about the post-death, pre-funeral sliver of time. The time when there's a dead body in a house that just a moment ago housed an alive body. The coroners are on their way, but they have to get into cars and drive to where the dead body is. I never thought about that.

So, we walked in before the coroners and there was the body that used to be grandpa. I was so stunned by it all, I didn't think to shield it from my children and I didn't really know what to do or where to go. I just kind of stood there.

When we had been at the house for a while, I found myself beside the deathbed and I did something I'd never done before. I held my grandpa's hand.

I loved my grandpa, but he just wasn't a hand-holding person. He was a faithful man who loved Jesus, just not the cuddly type.

But as I stood by his vacated body and grabbed his hand, already stiff and cold, I was overcome by how close I felt to him, for the first time. I imagined him in his perfectly functioning glorified body, and was overcome by the reality that soon, my glorified body, free of barriers and fear, might run and jump into his arms, crying tears of joy and disbelief.

Grandpa taught my mom that Jesus is the hope of the world. And she taught me. And I'm teaching my three girls—in English and in ASL—that Jesus is the hope of the world. And Jesus is the reason we're not constantly falling apart over deaths in the family and bad news and hard days.

Jesus is the reason we have joy. Jesus is our source of peace.

My grandpa was known for a lot of things. He was a great gymnastics coach and P.E. teacher. He served in the military. He was in vaudeville. He was a faithful husband for sixty years . . . but the legacy he left, to me, is that he taught our family about the forever hope we have in God.

The night of his death, when I was finally alone, trying to go to sleep, fear crept in. It is always looking for a chance to do that. But the Holy Spirit whispered to me, "There is no fear in love; instead, perfect love drives out fear, because fear involves punishment. So the one who fears is not complete in love" (1 John 4:18).

Jesus loves my grandpa perfectly—the same way He loves me and everyone I shared a van with as we drove around the cemetery on that weird Tuesday in April. We were able to laugh and sing and make jokes the day the patriarch of our family died. Why? Because he didn't die. That day, he started living. And soon, we will too. And it will be the funnest day ever.

GRIEVING AT THE BIRTHDAY PARTY

Death can even make birthdays sad. At what age does that start happening?

My kids wake up making euphoric shrieking sounds every day of their birth month leading up to THE day. Grown-ups don't do that. When I was little, I spent each entire birth-week skipping and laughing and expecting the people of the world to treat me like a champion. This year, I ate frozen yogurt and felt like a champion largely because I didn't cry.

Why is that? Why is it that the happiest day of the year for children can be one of the most difficult days of the year for adults? I think it is because, at some point, you become aware of death. Birthdays happen and death days happen, too. And at some point, you realize life isn't all candles and cake and that brokenness and loss are real. That's scary.

I was thinking about this the day my youngest, my little Dew, who is actually named Brooklyn, turned one. I remember staring at her little face as it studied the balloons and thinking, *I'm happy, but I'm also grieving. Brooklyn is one step closer to experiencing heartbreak and loss.*

I'm thankful that her mind and body are working well enough for her to need me less, but I'm also mourning. Every milestone moves her farther away from being my little baby.

I'm excited to celebrate her cuteness and her wobbly steps and I can't wait to watch her make a mess of her cupcake, but I can't ignore the fact that, someday she will hurt. Someday she will grieve.

Brooklyn isn't named Brooklyn because of the borough. My husband and I love the name, but we have no special relationship with New York City.

When I looked up the meaning of Brooklyn, I was floored. Brooklyn comes from the Dutch word *Breuckelen*, which means "from the land of the broken."

So we named her Brooklyn Hope.

This world is broken and bringing a baby into a world full of so much evil is terrifying. But there is hope in the land of the broken.

And, again, that's the incredible thing about being a Christian; the underlying sadness and fear that accompany every happy moment is really a myth. It's a lie! Jesus makes death and brokenness and grief (top tier scary right there) temporary.

My sister-in-law just had her own birthday and my husband asked her if she felt old. Her answer was beautiful. She answered, not like a child who doesn't yet know that death is real, but like a child of God who knows that death isn't final. She said, "I'm going to live forever. How can I feel old?"

Truth.

I want to live like eternal life is a reality . . . because it is.

Brooklyn Hope, our Dewy, is a bubbly preschooler now, and she likes the color blue and when my grandpa died, she thought that simply meant he went somewhere else. And we grown-ups have the tendency to smile sadly and shake our heads and shudder in fear at the thought of our own loved ones passing. We live like death is final, when three-year-old Dewy is actually the one who's right. Death is not final. For a Christian, death really is going somewhere else. Going somewhere, as Paul puts it "far better" (Phil. 1:23).

ANOTHER GRANDPA NAMED BERTHUL

Brandon's grandfather died shortly after mine did. He left a house and some acres in Illinois that the family is selling. But, after his death, while it was still in the family, we took a little family trip over there. Over to "Grandpa's house."

It was the first time we'd been there since we went for his funeral the year before. And he wasn't there. It was sad and it was emptier, but it was also still full of life. Ever brought me a bright bouquet of wildflowers tied with grass and we all ate the pears that we picked off the tree.

Grandpa Bert's legacy was woven into every part of that place. It was beautiful and "country." The girls spent a day being wild and making fairy houses.

And little Dewy was anxious to know when Grandpa would come back from heaven so he could see her pretty new dress.

And we missed Grandpa when she said that. We still do. What a guy.

But his death doesn't sting, because he spent his life loving Jesus on that land, and we know we'll see him again soon and Dewy will twirl and he'll smile at her in her dress and say, "You are a dandy!"

My little Brooklyn might not know it yet, that she lives in the land of the broken. But, she's figuring it out, and as she does, I get to tell her about this thrilling hope she can have because Jesus broke the curse of death when He walked out of the grave. Because He resurrected, we will too. Brokenness won't last forever. This is true. And believing that truth can shift our heart posture from fear of all the things, fear of the scariest things, fear of even death, to profound peace.

WHEN YOU DIE

There are things you can do to help subdue the anxiety caused by living in this scary place. But, the only way to have a soul that is deeply at peace, a soul that doesn't fear death, is to believe that the Bible is true.

The only way to really rest is by believing the gospel.

> He will destroy death forever. The Lord GOD will wipe away the tears from every face and remove his people's disgrace from the whole earth, for the LORD has spoken. On that day it will be said, "Look, this is our God; we have waited for him, and he has saved us. This is the LORD, we have waited for him. Let us rejoice and be glad in his salvation." (Isa. 25:8–9)

You've made it this far into the book, so you're probably hoping now for a take-away. So, here's one. Believe those words you just read. Those words of old, from the prophet, Isaiah, who knew the gospel before the gospel was even fulfilled. How did he have the peace before the Peace was made flesh? Why did he know it before it even happened? Because he knew God, Isaiah saw Him, and somehow lived, and he knew God could do what He said He would do. And what did He say He would do?

He. Will. Destroy. Death. Forever.

We are all waiting together for Him to do that. Waiting in this scary place. And when that fear overtakes us, when it all feels too much, when we want to have the peace and we remember the words of God, but we still feel the pain of the scary things, we remember this: our fears are not forever. The only thing our fears will have forever is their own destruction.

HE WILL DESTROY DEATH FOREVER.

Nothing sad or uncomfortable or uncertain or scary that you are going through right now is going to last forever. None of it.

Death does not have the final word. God does. And the Word of God has a name—Jesus.

> The Word became flesh and dwelt among us. We observed his glory, the glory as the one and only Son from the Father, full of grace and truth. (John 1:14)

A DEATH IN MY LIFE THAT JESUS REDEEMED

I don't know whether the two babies I miscarried were boys or girls. I'm guessing girls because I'm definitely a girl mom. But who knows?

I don't know what it will look like when I go to heaven. I don't know if I'll see my unborn children there or if I'll know they're them. I don't understand every bit of why they died, why I never got to meet them, or why other terrible things happen.

But God's given me the grace to see His hand, His redemption in their stories. Especially, the second one— "cancer baby."

I didn't know it then, but that weird summer in 2013 that I got pregnant right at the first hint of fall and had my second traumatic miscarriage, another little baby was born in China and abandoned. In the late summer of 2013, I lost my baby. And Joy was born.

Now, let's be clear: I'm not saying one child can replace another. Any parent knows that's not true. What I'm saying is that while broken things happen in this world, good things happen, too.

I can't comprehend God's sovereignty and the powerful ways He redeems what's broken. I can't wrap my mind around the reality that my daughter, my Joy, never knew the love of a family until she was almost four years old. I can't understand how God loved Joy so much that He shook us up and poured His love for her into our hearts in such obvious ways that it took away our fears.

I can't understand it. But I'm so thankful for it.

And now, I get to kiss her little face every day and tell her that she is loved and delighted in and ours forever.

There's redemption. Beauty for ashes. And God does things like this all the time.

Death is a thing that looms, but new life keeps coming. Babies are born. Sin is overcome. Addiction is renounced. Families are restored.

God is in the business of bringing dead things to life and creating new life where nothing could grow. Can you see it in your life? Can you look at your greatest pain points and see God's hand in it? I can. Not in everything, but in more things each day.

In life and in death, we have Christ. In life and in death, we are God's because of Christ and we are as impossible to keep in a grave as He was.

> "How strange this fear of death is! We are never frightened at a sunset." —George MacDonald

WHEN YOUR FEELINGS ARE TRYING TO KILL YOU

I like laughing, so I'm a big fan of the satirical Christian website, *The Babylon Bee,* and was thrilled to come across a beautiful and very non-satirical piece on anxiety written by the funny website's creator, Adam Ford, who battles anxiety himself. In his article titled "Some Things You Should Know about Christians Who Struggle with Anxiety," he writes:

> The gospel is everything to us. We live a life in which our feelings actively try to kill us. It's a strange existence. We know better than most that feelings can be filthy, stinking liars. While subjective feelings try to do us in, the objective truth of the gospel is what sustains us. It's our life raft. The fact that God chose us before the foundation of

the world, sent His Son to die on a cross for us, taking upon Himself the punishment for our sins, granting us eternal life in perfect bliss with Him in heaven—this is what sustains us through many dark times.

I don't know how I could go on without this truth sustaining me. This is the anchor of our soul: That our status before God is secure because *it's not dependent on our turbulent feelings, it's dependent on the finished work of Christ*, and when God looks at us, even when we're being smothered by a wet anxiety blanket, He sees a beloved child, perfectly clothed in the full righteousness of Jesus Christ. When you know we're struggling, send us a little reminder of the beautiful truth of the gospel. It might be a blessing bigger than you know. Tell us what Christ has done. Tell us "it is finished." Tell us what He accomplished on our behalf.[11]

I love that I have what Adam has. I love that God's shown me how to let go of my old "wet anxiety blanket" in light of the "it is finished" gospel. Despite the reality of a physical earthly death and feelings that propel us to obsess about it and be afraid, we have the gospel. We have the truth. We have the hope. We have the forever way to God through Jesus.

Jesus told him, "I am the way, the truth, and the life. No one comes to the Father except through me." (John 14:6)

Because of the finished work of Christ, we have access to real peace. Peace that doesn't go away when homes and grandfathers and appendixes do. Peace that isn't dependent on what has happened yesterday or what might happen tomorrow. Peace that puts death in its place.

PEACE ON HILTIBIDAL FARM

When I started writing this book, I was a city girl through and through. Big cities and big cities only, thank you very much. We've talked about this. In a city, you're a quick yelp from a hospital. You're an exaggerated wave from a taxi extraction. There's likely a police officer patrolling your neighborhood right around the corner.

Out in the country, who knows what can happen? That's what I used to think.

But I married a man who loves the country, and back when we visited Grandpa Bert's land a few years ago, before I even finished the sentence, "You know, Brandon, maybe land and chickens and country life aren't so bad after all . . ." he'd put our townhouse on the market. We're trying to buy a farm right this second.

As you read this book, I may very well be feeding chickens and donkeys. How does one do that? I have no idea. We'll have to YouTube that jank.

But this is something that my Brandon has always been into. He grew up hunting and fishing and out in the wild, admiring his grandparents who lived off the land. He says it is peaceful and worshipful and that it has the feeling of forever in it.

He emailed me this poem the other day, and I haven't been able to get it out of my head.

The Peace of Wild Things

By Wendell Berry

When despair for the world grows in me
and I wake in the night at the least sound
in fear of what my life and my children's
    lives may be,
I go and lie down where the wood drake
Rests in his beauty on the water, and the
    great heron feeds.
I come into the peace of wild things,
Who do not tax their lives with
    forethought
Of grief. I come into the presence of still
    water,
And I feel above me the day-blind stars
Waiting with their light. For a time
I rest in the grace of the world and I am
    free.[12]

Peace isn't found in where we live. Peace isn't found, not the lasting kind, in the suburb or the forest. Peace isn't found in the new job or the negative biopsies.

Perfect peace is found in Jesus, and in Him we can rest like the heron, "who do not tax their lives with forethought of grief." Only we have a level better than the bird. We don't rest because of ignorance; we rest because of victory.

And we don't need to move out into the boonies to find it, though; as I said, as you read this book, I may very well be making clothes for my children out of old curtains with cows on them. All we need to do to remember our place and grab our peace is seek the things above the field or above the street and above the sky, no matter how many townhouse complexes are in the way.

> So if you have been raised with Christ, seek the things above, where Christ is, seated at the right hand of God. Set your minds on things above, not on earthly things. For you died, and your life is hidden with Christ in God. When Christ, who is your life, appears, then you also will appear with him in glory. (Col. 3:1–4)

Here's some crazy news. We already have died. "For you died and your life is hidden with Christ in God."

Galatians 2:20 says that we have been "crucified with Christ." Dead. That's not bad news for the fearful. It's good news. Our failures and fumbles and fears are hidden in that death with Christ in God. The cross covers all our sin and all our doubt and all our fear—past, present, and future. Forever.

BE A PREACHER

Preach that truth to yourself. All the time. Preach this impossibly good news to your heart and to your friends and get friends who will preach it to you.

Get the Bible in your face and in your ears and on your lips. Remind yourself, rhythmically and beautifully, of the hope you have for life after death and abundant life between now and then by remembering what Jesus did. And remembering what He still does.

Do you know somebody who talks in Bible verses? There was a family I was in a small group with a few years ago that I describe this way. They were so full of the Word of God that it spilled out of them in every conversation.

The years I spent being in their lives coincided with years that my fears drifted into the background. So call that person who knows God's Word. Text your friend that is marked by peace. Get into their lives and let their lives spill into yours.

We walk and we pray and we hold each other up and we see the scary things and live through the scary things and pray God's Word over the scary things and we come to the other side and shake our heads and pinch ourselves and say, "Man, oh man. Look at this thing the Lord has done. Jesus really was enough again."

That's what we can say now and that's what we'll be saying for all eternity—maybe holding hands, maybe with our grandpas, definitely circled around a throne. And that is where our Savior will sit. In His "Ruler of the Universe" throne. And we'll be with Him, and everything scary will already be dead and gone forever and ever.

It's actually a little emotional for me to end this book. It's funny. I'm sitting outside of the Silver Sneakers Synchronized Swim class at the YMCA right now. I'm not even kidding. And I'm trying to control the ugly cry that's threatening me as I sit here and marvel at what God has done in my life and what I know He can do in yours.

A long time ago, I was five years old and fighting through the very intense and real fear of what I still say was the ugliest first day of school outfit ever worn. And now, I'm in my thirties and sometimes I hear about a child lost to cancer or a split-second, life-ending car accident and I feel the terror of death trying to sink its teeth into me. And sometimes, I feel strong and the power of the gospel floods my mind and I float above it all in the peace of Christ. But other times, I don't float. Other times, I fight for breath and I don't know what to say to make the scary thoughts go away, and all I can say is "Jesus."

But if you only have one word, that's the one. He is the One. Cross Bearer. Past Forgeter. Fear Crusher. Death Destroyer. Friend of Sinners. Friend of *Fearers*. Jesus.

Whether you're floating above your fears or wrestling through them today, Jesus lives. Your fears are not forever.

Jesus lives. Jesus loves. Jesus saves. And Jesus isn't afraid for you. Jesus has a word for you. Jesus simply says, "Fear not."

He doesn't offer you a life with nothing to be afraid of. He offers you Himself. Yesterday. Today. Forever.

> "How sweet the name of Jesus sounds,
> in a believer's ear! It soothes his sorrows,
> heals his wounds, and drives away his fear."
> —John Newton

ABOUT THE AUTHOR

Scarlet Hiltibidal is a very professional wife and mother to her family in Middle Tennessee. She loves sign language with her daughters, nachos by herself, writing for her friends, and learning to be a pretend-farmer with her husband. She treasures the freedom of resting in the work of Jesus and hopes to help others rest as well.

NOTES

1. Charles Haddon Spurgeon, *God Always Cares* (Shawnee, KS: Gideon House Books, 2017), 33.

2. http://biblehub.com/commentaries/mhc/1_john/3.htm

3. https://www.desiringgod.org/topics/fear-anxiety

4. Rick Warren, *Purpose Driven Life* (Grand Rapids, MI: Zondervan, 2002).

5. C. S. Lewis, *The Lion, the Witch, and the Wardrobe* (1950; repr., New York: HarperCollins, 2009), 77.

6. https://www.desiringgod.org/articles/the-british-candle

7. John Piper, *The Misery of Job and the Mercy of God* (Wheaton, IL: Crossway Books, 2002), 14–15.

8. Sermon "Herein Is Love" in *The Complete Works of C. H. Spurgeon*, Volume 42, Sermons 2446–2497 (Harrington, DE: Delmarva Publications, 2013).

9. https://www.desiringgod.org/articles/paul-i-am-content -with-weakness

10. https://www.desiringgod.org/articles/does-fear-belong-in -the-christians-life

11. https://www.challies.com/articles/some-things-you-should -know-about-christians-who-struggle-with-anxiety/

12. Wendell Berry, "The Peace of Wild Things" in *Openings: Poems* (1968).